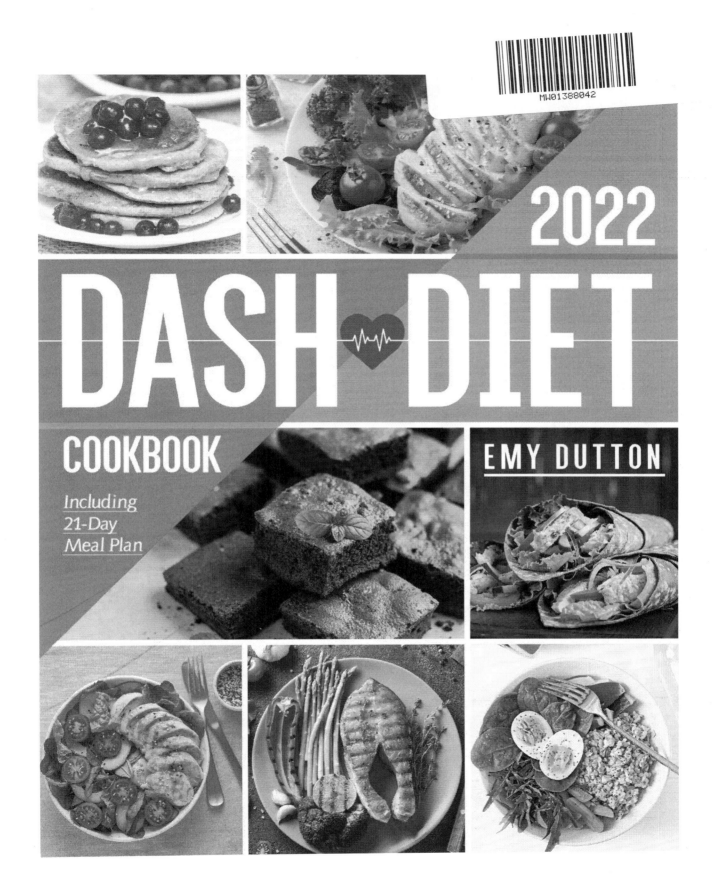

Copyright © - Emy Dutton. All rights reserved.

The content contained within this book may not be reproduced, duplicated or transmitted without direct written permission from the author or the publisher.

Under no circumstances will any blame or legal responsibility be held against the publisher, or author, for any damages, reparation, or monetary loss due to the information contained within this book. Either directly or indirectly.

Legal Notice:

This book is copyright protected. This book is only for personal use. You cannot amend, distribute, sell, use, quote or paraphrase any part, or the content within this book, without the consent of the author or publisher.

Disclaimer Notice:

Please note the information contained within this document is for educational and entertainment purposes only. All effort has been executed to present accurate, up to date, and reliable, complete information. No warranties of any kind are declared or implied. Readers acknowledge that the author is not engaging in the rendering of legal, financial, medical or professional advice. The content within this book has been derived from various sources. Please consult a licensed professional before attempting any techniques outlined in this book.

By reading this document, the reader agrees that under no circumstances is the author responsible for any losses, direct or indirect, which are incurred as a result of the use of information contained within this document, including, but not limited to, errors, omissions, or inaccuracies.

Table of Contents

- INTRODUCTION 9
- WHAT IS THE DASH DIET? 11
- BENEFITS OF THE DASH DIET 11
- WHAT TO EAT AND AVOID ON DASH DIET 12
  - Grain Products 12
  - Vegetables 13
  - Fruits and Berries 13
  - Dairy 13
  - Meat and Poultry 14
  - Fish and Seafood 15
  - Nuts, Seeds, and Legumes 15
  - Fats and Oils 15
  - Sweets 16
  - Alcohol and Caffeine 16
- TOP 10 TIPS FOR DASH DIET 12
- 21 DAY MEAL PLAN 17
- RECIPES 18
  - Breakfast 20
    - Mango Pineapple Green Smoothie 21
    - Antioxidant Smoothie Bowl 21
    - Apple Oats 21
    - Asparagus Omelet Tortilla Wrap 22
    - Buckwheat Crepes 22
    - Morning Glory Smoothie 23
    - Peach Avocado Smoothie 23
    - Peanut Butter & Banana Oatmeal 23
    - Dark Chocolate Walnut Bars 24
    - Whole Grain Pancakes 24
    - Granola Parfait 25
    - Curry Tofu Scramble 25
    - Scallions Omelet 25
    - Breakfast Almond Smoothie 26
    - Fruits and Rice Pudding 26
    - Blueberry Date Muffins 26
    - Broccoli Cheese Egg Muffins 27
    - Greek Breakfast Scramble 27
    - Bean Frittata 28
    - Peach Pancakes 28
    - Breakfast Splits 29
    - Banana Pancakes 29
    - Mushroom Thyme Frittata 30
    - Roasted Root Vegetable Hash 30
    - Hash Brown Vegetable Breakfast Casserole 31
    - Sweet Potato Pancakes with Maple Yogurt 31
    - Whole-Grain Flax Waffles with Strawberry Purée 32
    - Blueberry Waffles 33
    - Apple Pancakes 33
    - Egg Toasts 34
    - Sweet Yogurt with Figs 34
    - Very Berry Muesli 34
    - Veggie Quiche Muffins 35
    - Sweet Millet Congee 35
    - Summer Breakfast Quinoa Bowls 36
    - Red Velvet Pancakes with Cream Cheese Topping 36
    - Vanilla Toasts 37
    - Raspberry Yogurt 37
    - Salsa Eggs 37
    - Fruit Scones 38
  - Side Dishes 20
    - Sautéed Swiss Chard 40
    - Asian Style Asparagus 40
    - Aromatic Cauliflower Florets 40
    - Brussel Sprouts Mix 41
    - Braised Baby Carrot 41
    - Acorn Squash With Apples 42
    - Asparagus with Horseradish Dip 42
    - Grilled Tomatoes 42
    - Parsley Celery Root 43
    - Garlic Black Eyed Peas 43
    - Corn Relish 44
    - Braised Artichokes 44
    - Spiced Eggplant Slices 44
    - Lentil Sauté 45
    - Italian Style Zucchini Coins 45
    - Brussels Sprouts with Shallots & Lemon 46
    - Chili-Lime Grilled Pineapple 46
    - Light Wild Rice 47
    - Mashed Potato with Avocado 47
    - Baked Herbed Carrot 47
    - Grilled Pineapple Rings 48
    - Chickpea Stew 48
    - Quinoa Bowl 48
    - Sautéed Celery Stalk 49
    - Asparagus in Sauce 49
    - Thyme Potatoes 49
    - Sesame Seeds Brussel Sprouts 50
    - Potato Pan 50
    - Cauliflower Bake 50

- *Parsley Broccoli* 51
- *Tomato Brussel Sprouts* 51

SOUPS 39
- *Summer Berry Soup* 54
- *Green Beans Soup* 54
- *Turkey Soup* 54
- *Beef Soup* 55
- *Cream of Wild Rice Soup* 55
- *Curried Cream of Tomato Soup with Apples* 56
- *Potato Fennel Soup* 56
- *Tomato Green Bean Soup* 57
- *Asparagus Cream Soup* 57
- *Pasta Soup* 58
- *Black Beans Soup* 58
- *Carrot Soup* 59
- *Cucumber and Melon Soup* 59
- *Green Detox Soup* 59
- *Low Sodium Vegetable Soup* 60
- *Pumpkin Cream Soup* 60
- *Zucchini Noodles Soup* 61
- *Chicken Oatmeal Soup* 61
- *Celery Cream Soup* 62
- *Buckwheat Soup* 62
- *Parsley Soup* 62
- *Tomato Bean Soup* 63
- *Red Kidney Beans Soup* 63
- *Pork Soup* 64
- *Curry Soup* 64
- *Yellow Onion Soup* 64
- *Garlic Soup* 65
- *Poultry Soup* 65
- *Roasted Tomatoes Soup* 66
- *Yogurt Soup* 66

SALADS 53
- *Salad Skewers* 68
- *Asian Style Cobb Salad* 68
- *Tomato Salad* 68
- *Cheese & Steak Salad* 69
- *Corn Salad with Spinach* 69
- *Shredded Beef Salad* 69
- *Tangerine and Edamame Salad* 70
- *Chicken Salad in Jars* 70
- *Farro Salad* 71
- *Warm Lentil Salad* 71
- *Grilled Cod and Blue Cheese Salad* 72
- *Tabbouleh Salad* 72
- *Fattoush* 72
- *Couscous Salad* 73
- *Bean Salad with Balsamic Vinaigrette* 73
- *Warm Rice & Pintos Salad* 74
- *Celeriac Salad* 74
- *Crunchy Lettuce Salad* 75
- *Herbed Melon Salad* 75
- *Spring Greens Salad* 75
- *Apple Salad with Figs & Almonds* 76
- *Asian Vegetable Salad* 76
- *Tuna Salad* 77
- *Fish Salad* 77
- *Apple lettuce salad* 77
- *Salmon Salad* 78
- *Arugula Salad with Shallot* 78
- *Berry Salad with Shrimps* 78

POULTRY 67
- *BBQ Basil Turkey Burgers* 80
- *Basic Roast Chicken Breast* 80
- *Chicken Skillet* 81
- *Turkey Stir-Fry* 81
- *Chicken and Low-fat Goat Cheese Bowl* 82
- *Chicken Chop Suey* 82
- *Classic Poached Chicken* 83
- *Chicken Mediterranean with Artichokes and Rosemary* 83
- *Chicken Packets* 84
- *Herbed Chicken Breast* 84
- *Chinese Chicken with Bok Choy and Garlic* 85
- *Chicken with Mushroom Cacciatore Sauce* 85
- *Chicken and Vegetables Wraps* 86
- *Sesame Shredded Chicken* 86
- *Chicken Piccata* 87
- *Lean Chicken Thighs* 87
- *Blackened Chicken* 87
- *Chicken and Apple Curry* 88
- *"Moo Shu" Chicken and Vegetable Wraps* 89
- *Roast Turkey Breast with Root Vegetables, Lemon, and Garlic Cloves* 89
- *Grilled Chicken Fillets* 90
- *Oregano Turkey Tenders* 91
- *Turkey Chili* 91
- *Turkey Bake* 92
- *Turkey Meatloaf* 92
- *Turkey Burgers* 92
- *Turkey-Spinach Meatballs with Tomato Sauce* 93
- *Cajun Turkey Burgers with Pickled Red Onions* 94
- *Turkey Mini Meat Loaf with Dijon Glaze* 94

- Curry Chicken Wings 95
- Basil Stuffed Chicken Breast 96
- Tomato Chicken Stew 96
- Turkey Mix 96
- Onion Chicken 97
- Spiced Turkey Fillet 97
- Balsamic Vinegar Chicken 97
- Citrus Chicken 98
- Glazed Chicken 98
- Turkey Mushrooms 98
- Spring Chicken Mix 99
- Peach Turkey 99

BEEF AND PORK 79
- Herbs de Provence Pork Chops 101
- Curry Pork Chops 101
- Pork Roast with Orange Sauce 101
- Southwestern Steak 102
- Tender Pork Medallions 102
- Garlic Pork Meatballs 103
- Fajita Pork Strips 103
- Curry-Rubbed Sirloin with Peanut Dipping Sauce 103
- Sirloin, Shiitake, and Asparagus Stir-Fry 104
- Beef and Mushrooms with Sour Cream-Dill Sauce 105
- Pepper Pork Tenderloins 105
- Spiced Beef 105
- Tomato Beef 106
- Hoisin Pork 106
- Sage Beef Loin 107
- Spiced Roast Eye of Round 107
- Beef Fajitas with Two Peppers 107
- Ground Sirloin and Pinto Chili 108
- Beef Chili 109
- Celery Beef Stew 109
- Beef Skillet 109
- Hot Beef Strips 110
- Ground Turkey Fiesta 110
- Sloppy Joe 110
- Beef and Bulgur Meat Loaf 111
- Beef Ragù with Broccoli Ziti 112
- Turmeric Meatloaf 112
- Beef Casserole 112
- Garlic Steak 113
- Ham Casserole 113
- Beef Ranch Steak 114
- Pork Casserole 114
- Melted Beef Bites 114
- Pork Sliders Meat 115
- Beef Saute 115
- Light Shepherd Pie 115
- Meat&Mushrooms Bowl 116
- Tandoori Beef 116
- Oregano Pork Tenderloin 117
- Baked Beef Tenders 117
- Pork Stuffed Peppers 117

FISH AND SEAFOOD 100
- Spicy Cajun Salmon Bake 120
- Salmon with Grapefruit, Avocado, and Fennel Salad 120
- Rice Paella with Shrimp and Asparagus 121
- Limes and Shrimps Skewers 122
- Crusted Salmon with Horseradish 122
- Cucumber and Seafood Bowl 122
- Fish Tacos 123
- Tuna and Pineapple Kebob 123
- Paprika Tilapia 124
- Herbed Sole 124
- Shrimp Tacos with Lime-Cilantro Slaw 124
- Rosemary Salmon 125
- Tuna Stuffed Zucchini Boats 125
- Baked Cod 126
- Basil Halibut 126
- Tilapia Veracruz 126
- Lemon Swordfish 127
- Spiced Scallops 127
- Shrimp Putanesca 127
- Curry Snapper 128
- Grouper with Tomato Sauce 128
- Braised Seabass 128
- Five-Spices Sole 129
- Clams Stew 129
- Salmon in Capers 129
- Mustard Tuna Salad 130
- Shallot Tuna 130
- Cod Relish 131
- Mint Cod 131
- Dill Steamed Salmon 131
- Cod in Tomatoes 132
- Spinach Halibut 132
- Paprika Tuna Steaks 132
- Grilled Tilapia 132
- Cod in Orange Juice 133
- Tomato Halibut Fillets 133
- Salmon with Basil and Garlic 133

- Mustard Arctic Char 134
- Cod in Yogurt Sauce 134
- Parsley Trout 134

VEGAN AND VEGETARIAN 119
- Mushroom Florentine... 137
- Bean Hummus 137
- Hasselback Eggplant 137
- Vegetarian Kebabs 138
- White Beans Stew 138
- Vegetarian Lasagna 139
- Carrot Cakes 139
- Vegan Chili 139
- Aromatic Whole Grain Spaghetti 140
- Chunky Tomatoes.. 140
- Baby minted carrots.. 140
- Baked Falafel 141
- Paella 141
- Mushroom Cakes 142
- Glazed Eggplant Rings... 142
- Sweet Potato Balls 142
- Chickpea Curry 143
- Quinoa Bowl.. 143
- Vegan Meatloaf 144
- Loaded Potato Skins.. 144

DESSERTS 136
- Sweet Fruit Salad 147
- Berry Sundae 147
- Grilled Apricots with Cinnamon 147
- Peaches with Ricotta Stuffing and Balsamic Glaze 148
- Beans Brownies 148
- Avocado Mousse 149
- Fruit Kebabs 149
- Vanilla Soufflé 149
- Strawberries in Dark Chocolate........................... 150
- Fruit Bowl 150
- Grilled Pineapple 150
- Red Sangria 151
- Baked Apples Stuffed with Cranberries and Walnuts 151
- Buttermilk Panna Cotta with Fresh Berries 152
- Berry Smoothie.. 152
- Grilled Peaches 153
- Stuffed Fruits 153
- Oatmeal Cookies 153
- Baked Apples... 154
- Peach Crumble 154
- Cantaloupe and Mint Ice Pops 154
- Peach and Granola Parfaits 155
- Banana Saute 156
- Rhubarb Muffins 156
- Poached Pears... 156
- Lemon Pie.. 157
- Fresh Strawberries with Chocolate Dip 157
- Cardamom Pudding 157
- Banana Bread.. 158

Introduction

This book aims to provide DASH diet recipes that are easy to understand and can be prepared easily and quickly. The last decade has seen an exponential increase in people opting for the DASH diet. The Dietary Approaches to Stop Hypertension diet is becoming a household name as more and more people realize its potential to control hypertension and high blood sugar. The DASH diet typically includes foods low in sodium and rich in potassium, calcium, and magnesium. The diet also recommends the person to stay away from processed carbohydrates, carbonated drinks, and sugar.

Given the current lifestyle, getting exhausted and falling for an unhealthy diet is not uncommon. This has led to an increase in young adults contracting diabetes and blood sugar disorders. Heart problems previously seen in older people have now found a new host among those in their 30s. This has dramatically increased the need to find avenues to go back to healthy living. Thus, many people are now planning to use the DASH diet as one of the methods to reduce such disorders. This cookbook is the perfect supplement you will find to combat high blood sugar and hypertension and aims to advise the expert and help a beginner follow the recipes written in a self-explanatory and straightforward method. It provides a vast menu spread over 21 days. This includes breakfast, lunch, and dinner recipes, helping you manage the entire month.

The 21-day meal plan was well thought out and created considering people's busy lifestyles. Meals also align with the body's daily nutritional requirements and ensure that the person does not miss out on any essential supplements. The meal plan helps track growth and manage meals. If someone cooks for you, they should follow the meal plan and avoid the hassle of calculating calorie intake.

People who cannot indulge in daily cooking can prepare extra food and sit in the refrigerator. This will not only save you time, but also prevent you from straying from the meal plan. Also, the reader can plan and store food at their convenience.

A lot of effort has gone into listing recipes that will help you manage your calorie count and not compromise the taste of your food. Usually, people planning to control blood sugar focus on simple, tasteless foods. While some may stick to such a routine, most of us give up in the absence of taste. The recipes in this cookbook are intended to improve your health by enjoying different foods.

These DASH diet recipes will help you control your blood sugar and let you enjoy the entire process, probably for the first time.

What is the DASH Diet?

The DASH Diet involves a healthy eating plan to treat or prevent hypertension (also known as high blood pressure). Hypertension affects more than one billion people worldwide, and this number is still increasing. Hypertension leads to different heart diseases, including congestive heart failure, kidney disease, and stroke. Researchers have noted that hypertension is less common in people who eat veggies or are vegetarian. The DASH Diet is not a vegetarian one but emphasizes consuming more fruits, vegetables, lean protein, and low-fat dairy products.

The U.S. National Institutes of Health created the DASH Diet to help people manage their blood pressure. The primary purpose of developing the diet was to lower or decrease the risks of high blood pressure without medication. The initial research results were impressive, showing that the DASH Diet not only helps reduce blood pressure but can be used as a first-line treatment of hypertension. Therefore, the DASH Diet is a natural way of treating high blood pressure without using medications.

With further research, the DASH Diet was also found to reduce the incidence of other diseases, such as cancer and diabetes. These results are why, since 2011, it has accomplished the #1 diet ranking in the U.S. News & World Report six years in a row. Recent studies have shown that those following the DASH Diet find their blood pressure drops within two weeks. According to the results, if people with high blood pressure followed the DASH Diet precisely, this could prevent around 400,000 deaths from cardiovascular disease over ten years. The

DASH Diet includes foods low in salt and rich in potassium, calcium, and magnesium. The diet minimizes foods that are high in sodium, saturated fat, and added sugars. It provides healthy alternatives to "junk food" and encourages people to avoid eating processed foods.

Benefits of DASH diet

The benefits of the DASH diet go beyond reducing hypertension and heart disease.

Controlling blood pressure: The force exerted on our blood vessels and organs when blood passes through them is a measure of blood pressure in the human body. When blood pressure increases beyond a certain level, it can lead to various bodily malfunctions, including heart failure.

Blood pressure is counted in two numbers: systolic pressure (pressure exerted in the blood vessels when the heart beats) and diastolic pressure (pressure exerted in the blood vessels when the heart is at rest). The average adult systolic blood pressure is less than 120 mmHg, while diastolic blood pressure is typically less than 80 mmHg. Anyone who exceeds these limits is said to have high blood pressure.

Restricting sodium intake and relying on vegetables, healthy fats, lean meats and fruits in the DASH diet significantly controls blood pressure. The less salt you consume, the lower your blood pressure will be. Effective use of the DASH diet can influence the systolic blood pressure by an average change of 12 mmHg and control the diastolic blood pressure by 5 mmHg. The DASH diet is not reserved for hypertension; it can also work well for people with normal blood pressure. The trick is to consume regular amounts of salt and the dietary recommendations given in the DASH diet.

Controls diabetes: The diet is very beneficial for people with type 2 diabetes.

Fights cancer risk: People who follow the DASH diet have a lower risk of colorectal and breast cancer.

Checks metabolic syndrome: The diet lower the risk of metabolic syndrome.

Heart diseases: The diet lower the risk of heart disease and stroke.

Weight loss: People with high blood pressure are recommended to keep their weight, as extra weight can result in health complications. Obesity, along with high blood pressure, can lead to heart and organ failure. With the help of the DASH diet, you can lower your blood pressure and reduce your weight at the same time. Credit for this goes to the healthy foods recommended in the DASH diet. It is recommended to reduce the number of daily calories to lose weight.

What to Eat and Avoid Diet

Grain Products

Use always whole grains because they are richer in nutrients and fiber. They are low-fat and can easily substitute cheese, cream and butter.

What to eat

- Quinoa
- Whole-grain breakfast
- cereals
- Bulgur
- Brown rice
- Rice cakes
- Oatmeal
- Popcorn

Eat occasionally

- Whole-wheat pasta
- Whole-wheat noodles

What to avoid

- White rice
- White bread
- Regular pasta

Vegetables

Vegetables are the richest source of potassium, fiber, vitamins, and magnesium. You can use vegetables as a side dish and as a topping, spread, or meat-free main dish substitute.

What to eat

- All fresh vegetables and greens
- Low-sodium canned vegetables

What to avoid

- Regular canned vegetables

Fruits and Berries

Fruits and berries have the same life benefits as vegetables. They are rich in vitamins and minerals. One more advantage of fruits and berries is their low-fat content. They can be a good substitute for sweets and snacks. Fruit peels contain the highest level of fiber and valuable nutrients compared to fruit pulp.

What to eat

- All fruits and berries (mango, pineapple, apple, pears, strawberries, raspberries, dates, apricots, etc.)

Eat occasionally

- Grapefruit
- Lemon
- Orange

What to avoid

- Sugar added canned
- fruits
- Coconut

Dairy

Dairy products are the primary source of D vitamins and calcium. The only restriction for followers of the dash diet is saturated and high-fat dairy products.

Note: you can substitute dairy products with cashew, nut, soy milk and almond.

What to eat

- Low-fat / fat-free milk/percent milk
- Low-fat or fat-free cheese
- Low-fat or fat-free yogurt
- Low-fat or fat-free frozen yogurt
- Low-fat or fat-free skim milk

Eat occasionally

- Low-fat buttermilk
- Low-fat cream

What to avoid

- Full-fat cheese
- Full-fat cream
- Full-fat yogurt
- Full-fat milk

Meat and Poultry

Meat is rich in iron, zinc, B vitamins and protein. There is a wide selection of recipes that will help you cook meat in many ways. You can grill, broil, roast or bake it, but anyways it will be delicious.

Note: avoid eating skin and fat from poultry and meat.

What to eat

- Skinless chicken wings
- Skinless chicken breast
- Skinless chicken thighs
- Chicken fillet
- Skinless drumsticks

Eat occasionally

- Eggs
- Lean cuts of red meat (lamb, pork, veal, beef)

What to avoid

- Bacon
- Fat cuts of meat
- Fat
- Pork belly

Fish and Seafood

All types of fish and seafood are accepted in the dash diet. The main benefits you will get from fish that is rich in omega-3 fatty acids. Below you will find the best choice of fish for the dash diet.

What to eat

- Tuna
- Salmon
- Herring

What to avoid

- Canned fish and seafood with high sodium content

Nuts, Seeds, and Legumes

This type of product is high in fiber, potassium, phytochemicals, magnesium, and proteins. It can also fight cancer and cardiovascular disease.
Legumes, nuts and seeds, and are high in calories and should be eaten in moderation. Add them in your salads or main dishes, and they will saturate the taste.

What to eat

- All types of legumes
- All types of seeds
- All types of nuts

Fats and Oils

The primary function of fats is to help absorb vitamins; however, the high amount of fats can lead to developing heart diseases, obesity, and diabetes.

According to the dash diet, your daily meal plan should include no more than 30% fat of your daily calories.

What to eat

- Vegetable oils
- Margarine

Eat occasionally

- Dressings
- mayonnaise
- Low-fat
- Light-salad

What to avoid

- Butter
- Lard
- Solid shortening
- Palm oil

Sweets

Crossing out all sweets from your daily diet is unnecessary, but it is essential to follow some of the dash diet's restrictions: choose sugar-free, low-fat/fat-free sweets or replace them with fruits and berries.

What to eat

- Fruit/berries sorbets
- Fruit ice
- Graham crackers
- Honey
- Sugar-free fruit jelly

Eat occasionally

- Hard candy
- Splenda
- Aspartame (NutraSweet,
- Equal)
- Agave syrup
- Maple syrup

What to avoid

- Biscuits
- Crackers
- Sweet junk food
- Cookies
- Table sugar
- Soda
- Unrefined sugar

Alcohol and Caffeine

You should limit alcohol to 2 drinks per day for men and up to 1 or fewer drinks for women.

Note: Alcohol and caffeine consumption may be prohibited if required by a medical examination.

Top 10 Tips for Dash Diet

1. **Walking is essential.**

Simple sports activities, walking or cycling, will strengthen the effect of the dash diet and help in weight loss.

The perfect combination to stabilize blood pressure is a minimum of 2 hours of walking and 30 minutes of exercise per week. If that sounds complicated, start with 1 hour of walking and 10 minutes of sports exercise; increase the load until you get your desired time.

2. **Don't change your life drastically.**

To not stress your body, change your eating habits step-by-step until you adjust them according to the dash diet plan.

3. **Create a food journal.**

It will help you realize how much food you eat per day and whether it is diet-friendly. Following such a journal should be regular. Rest assured that within a week, you will see a significant result in your attitude towards food.

4. **Make every meal green.**

Make it a rule to add a few green vegetables to every meal. This way you will provide a lot of fiber and potassium to your body.

5. **Be a vegan once per week.**

Limit your meat consumption and avoid eating meat once per week. Eat more beans, nuts, tofu, which are rich in proteins too.

6. **Fresh box.**

Make a box with fruits, vegetables, and rice cakes for your snack time. Such a box will help you avoid high-sodium fast food consumption.

7. **Food labels are helpful.**

Always read food labels before buying packaged or processed foods. By doing this, you can better control the level of the amount of sodium.

Notice that the low-sodium canned food should have less than 140mg of sodium per serving.

8. **Add spices.**

Such spices as rosemary, cayenne pepper, chili pepper, cilantro, dill, cinnamon, etc., can saturate the taste and make more delicious even non-salty meals.

9. Make your snack delicious.

People prefer different types of snacks. Not all of them adore fruits and vegetables. It can be difficult for them to switch on healthy food immediately. That's why make a list of your favorite products and eat them during the day like a snack. The food list will be appropriate until you get rid of all junk food from your diet.

10. Make a body examination every 2 months.

Some health problems can't be changed just by changing the food plan. The doctor's participation in your diet is essential. Make the entire body examination before starting a diet and then consult a doctor about any discomfort in your body or health every two months; it will allow following the diet in the most comfortable way for your health.

21 Day Meal Plan

B. Breakfast **L.** Lunch **D.** Dinner

DAY 1	DAY 2	DAY 3	DAY 4	DAY 5
B: Antioxidant Smoothie Bowl **L:** Vegetarian Lasagna **D:** Turkey Burgers	**B:** Morning Glory Smoothie **L:** Warm Lentil Salad **D:** Oregano Pork Tenderloin	**B:** Apple Oats **L:** Green Beans Soup **D:** Grilled Chicken Fillets	**B:** Breakfast Almond Smoothie **L:** Tomato Salad **D:** Spiced Beef	**B:** Blueberry Date Muffins **L:** Aromatic Whole Grain Spaghetti **D:** Salmon with Grapefruit, Avocado and Fennel Salad
DAY 6	**DAY 7**	**DAY 8**	**DAY 9**	**DAY 10**
B: Fruits and Rice Pudding **L:** Sweet Potato Balls **D:** Shallot Tuna	**B:** Dark Chocolate Walnut Bars **L:** Warm Rice and Pintos Salad **D:** Mint Cod	**B:** Peach Avocado Smoothie **L:** Chicken Oatmeal Soup **D:** Fish Tacos	**B:** Bean Frittata **L:** Zucchini Noodles Soup **D:** Baked Beef Tenders	**B:** Peach Pancakes **L:** Turkey Bake **D:** Herbed Sole
DAY 11	**DAY 12**	**DAY 13**	**DAY 14**	**DAY 15**
B: Egg Toasts	**B:** Very Berry Muesli **L:** Light Wild Rice	**B:** Vanilla Toasts **L:** Mashed Potato with Avocado	**B:** Raspberry Yogurt **L:** Quinoa Bowl	**B:** Fruit Scones **L:** Pasta Soup

L: Rice Paella with Shrimps and Asparagus **D:** Tomato Salad	**D:** Classic Poached Chicken	**D:** Pork Roast with Orange Sauce	**D:** Bean Hummus	**D:** Carrot Cakes
DAY 16	**DAY 17**	**DAY 18**	**DAY 19**	**DAY 20**
B: Salsa Eggs **L:** Vegetarian Lasagna **D:** Turkey Burgers	**B:** Apple Pancakes **L:** Poultry Soup **D:** Mushroom Florentine	**B:** Blueberry Waffles **L:** Warm Rice and Pintos Salad **D:** Mint Cod	**B:** Banana Pancakes **L:** Quinoa Bowl **D:** Garlic Steak	**B:** Breakfast Splits **L:** Crusted Salmon with Horseradish **D:** Tomato Salad
DAY 21				
B: Greek Breakfast Scramble **L:** Pork Soup **D:** Light Wild Rice				

RECIPES

Breakfast

Mango Pineapple Green Smoothie

Preparation Time: 3 min

Servings: 2

Ingredients:

- 1 cup frozen mango chunks
- 1 cup frozen pineapple chunks
- 1 cup fresh spinach or kale
- 1¼ cups orange juice
- ½ cup nonfat plain or vanilla Greek yogurt
- 1 tablespoon ground flaxseed
- 1 teaspoon granulated stevia

Directions:

1. Place all ingredients in the pitcher of a mixer. Blend until smooth.
2. Serve immediately

Per serving: Calories 213, Total Fat 2g, Sodium 44mg, Potassium 582mg, Total Carbohydrate 43g, Protein 9 g

---

Antioxidant Smoothie Bowl

Preparation Time: 17 min.

Servings: 1

Ingredients:

Smoothie:

- 2 tbsp. chia gel (see step 1)
- ½ medium frozen banana, cut into pieces
- ¾ cup cherries, frozen
- ½ cup coconut yogurt
- 1 tbsp. pure cocoa powder
- 1 tbsp. macadamia nut butter
- 1 cup fresh chard
- 1 teaspoon vanilla extract
- ½ cup unsweetened nut milk.
- 3-4 ice cubes

To serve:

- ½ tbsp. cocoa nibs
- Fresh berries
- Toasted macadamia nuts, roughly chopped
- ½ banana thinly sliced
- Dried goji berries

Directions:

1. Make your chia gel first – Mix ⅓cup chia seeds and 2 cups water well. An easy way to do this is to mix the ingredients in a jar and shake it for about 15 seconds. Let the gel rest for 1 minute, then shake/mix again and put it into the fridge for about 10 minutes until it forms a firm gel.
2. Then blend all the smoothie ingredients on high in a blender until you have a beautifully smooth, creamy smoothie. Be sure not to make it too fluid by adding the milk little by little.
3. Serve topped with the toppings of your choice arranged beautifully, with a sprinkle of cocoa powder to finish.
4. Eat immediately!

Per serving: 412 calories; 61g carbs; 20g protein; 13g fiber; 182mg sodium; 5mg cholesterol; 14g fat

---

Apple Oats

Preparation time: 5 min

Cooking time: 5 min

Servings: 2

Ingredients:

- ½ cup oats
- 1 cup of water
- 1 apple, chopped
- 1 teaspoon e.v.o. oil
- ½ teaspoon vanilla extract

Directions:

1. Pour the e.v.o. oil into the casserole dish and add the oats. Cook for 2 minutes, stirring constantly.
2. After this, add water and mix up.
3. Close the lid and cook the oats over low heat for 6 minutes.
4. After this, add the chopped apples and vanilla extract. Combine with the flour.

Per serving: 159 calories, 3g protein, carbs, 3.9g fat, 4.8g fiber, 0mg cholesterol, 6mg sodium, 196mg potassium.

Asparagus Omelet Tortilla Wrap

Preparation time: 20 min.

Servings: 1

Ingredients:

- Egg (1 whole large)
- Fat-free milk (1 tbsp.)
- Egg whites (2 large)
- Parmesan cheese - grated (2 tsp.)
- Black pepper (.125 or ⅛ tsp.)
- Fresh asparagus spears (4)
- Butter (1 tsp.)
- Green onion (1)
- Whole wheat tortilla (1 @ 8 inches - warmed)

Directions:

1. Whisk the eggs with the milk, pepper, and parmesan until incorporated.
2. Spritz a skillet with cooking spray and heat it using the medium temperature setting.
3. Add and sauté the asparagus (3-4 min.). Remove the asparagus from the pan.
4. Use the same pan to warm the butter using med-high heat.
5. Pour in the egg mixture. Cook the eggs, pushing them to the center until it's one layer and thickened.
6. Trim and slice the asparagus and chop the onion.
7. When eggs are thickened, spoon the green onion and asparagus on one side. Fold the omelet in half and serve in a tortilla.

Per serving: 319 calories, 28 g carbs, 13 g fat content, 21 g protein, 4 g sugar, 3 g fiber, 444 mg sodium

Buckwheat Crepes

Prep time: 8 min

Cooking time: 15 min

Servings: 6

Ingredients:

- 1 cup buckwheat flour
- 1/3 cup whole grain flour
- 1 egg, beaten
- 1 cup skim milk
- 1 teaspoon olive oil
- ½ teaspoon ground cinnamon

Directions:

1. In mixing bowl, mix all ingredients and whisk until smooth.

2. Heat the non-stick skillet on high heat for 3 minutes.
3. Using the ladle, pour the small amount of batter into the pan and flatten it into a crepe shape.
4. Cook it for 1 min and flip on another side. Cook it for 30 seconds more.
5. Repeat with remaining batter.

Per serving: 120 calories, 5.7g protein, 211g carbs, 2.2g fat, 2g fiber, 28mg cholesterol, 34mg sodium, 216mg potassium.

Morning Glory Smoothie

Preparation Time: 10 min

Servings: 2

Ingredients:

- 1 cup nonfat milk
- ½ cup 100% apple juice
- 2 tablespoons chopped walnuts
- 2 tablespoons unsweetened coconut flakes
- 2 frozen bananas
- 1 small carrot, peeled and chopped
- ½ teaspoon ground cinnamon
- ½ teaspoon pure vanilla extract
- ½ teaspoon granulated stevia
- 1 to 2 cups ice cubes

Directions:

1. Place the walnuts, milk, apple juice and coconut flakes in the pitcher of a blender. Let sit 5 minutes.
2. Add the pitcher to the frozen bananas, carrot, cinnamon, vanilla extract, stevia, and ice cubes. Purée until smooth.
3. Serve immediately.

Per serving: 276 Calories, 8g Total Fat, 72mg Sodium, 708mg Potassium, 46g Total Carbs, 6g Protein

Peach Avocado Smoothie

Preparation Time: 13 min

Servings: 2

Ingredients:

- 1½ cups frozen peaches
- 1½ cups nonfat milk
- 1 cup vanilla Greek yogurt
- 1 avocado, peeled and pitted
- 1 tablespoon ground flaxseed
- 1½ teaspoons granulated stevia
- 1 teaspoon pure vanilla extract
- 1 to 2 cups ice cubes

Directions:

1. Combine all the ingredients in a blender. Purée until smooth.
2. Serve immediately.

Per serving: 323 Calories, 15g Total Fat, 142mg Sodium, 186mg Potassium, 32g Total Carbs, 21g Protein

Peanut Butter & Banana Oatmeal

Preparation Time: 13 min

Cooking Time: 10 min

Servings: 6

Ingredients:

- 2 cups old-fashioned rolled oats
- 3½ cups water
- ½ cup natural peanut butter
- 3 tablespoons pure maple syrup
- ½ tablespoons ground cinnamon
- 1 teaspoon pure vanilla extract
- ½ teaspoon kosher or sea salt
- ½ cup nonfat milk
- 2 ripe bananas, peeled and sliced

Directions:

1. Transfer the oats and water to a medium saucepan and bring to a boil. Cook for about 5 minutes, stirring often, until the oats are soft.
2. Remove from heat and stir in peanut-butter, maple syrup, cinnamon, vanilla extract and salt until combined.
3. Divide oatmeal into bowls and add milk and sliced bananas.
4. Place leftovers in airtight microwave-safe containers and refrigerate for up to 5 days. Reheat in microwave at high intensity 1½ to 2 minutes.

Per serving: 298 Calories, 13g Total Fat, 304mg Sodium, 178mg Potassium, 39g Total Carbs, 9g Protein

Dark Chocolate Walnut Bars

Preparation Time: 65 min

Servings: 6

Ingredients:

- 2 cups chopped walnuts
- 2 cups unsweetened shredded coconut
- 12 pitted Medjool dates
- ½ cup dark cocoa powder
- ¼ cup melted coconut oil
- ¼ cup dark chocolate chips
- 3 tablespoons honey
- 1 teaspoon pure vanilla extract

Directions:

1. Prepare an 8-by-8-inch baking dish with baking paper.
2. Place all ingredients in the bowl of a food processor and pulse until a sticky dough forms. Transfer the dough to the prepared baking dish and spread it out evenly with the back of a spoon. Seal with plastic wrap and let cool for at least 3hours, until firm.
3. Pull up the sides of the parchment paper and transfer the bars to a cutting board. Slice into 12 equal sized squares.

Per serving: 375 Calories, 29g Total Fat, 50mg Sodium, 256mg Potassium, 34g Total Carbs, 5g Protein

Whole Grain Pancakes

Preparation time: 5 min

Cooking time: 10 min

Servings: 4

Ingredients:

- ½ teaspoon baking powder
- ¼ cup skim milk
- 1 cup whole-grain wheat flour
- 2 teaspoons liquid honey
- 1 teaspoon olive oil

Directions:

1. Mix up flour and baking powder in the bowl.

2. Add skim milk and olive oil. Whisk the mixture well.
3. Preheat non-stick pan and pour the small amount of batter inside in pancake shape. Cook for 2 minutes on each side or until pancake is golden brown.
4. Top the cooked pancakes with the liquid honey.

Per serving: 127 calories, 4.4g protein, 25.6g carbs, 1.7g fat, 3.7g fiber, 0mg cholesterol, 10mg sodium, 211mg potassium.

Granola Parfait

Preparation time: 10 min

Cooking time: 0 min

Servings: 2

Ingredients:

- ½ cup low-fat yogurt
- 4 tablespoons granola

Directions:

1. Put ½ tablespoon of granola in every glass.
2. Then add 2 tablespoons of low-fat yogurt.
3. Repeat steps until all ingredients are used.
4. Store the parfait in the refrigerator for up to 2-hours.

Per serving: 80 calories, 8g protein, 20.6g carbs, 8.1g fat, 2.8g fiber, 4mg cholesterol, 51mg sodium, 308mg potassium.

Curry Tofu Scramble

Preparation time: 10 min

Cooking time: 5 min

Servings: 3

Ingredients:

- 12 oz tofu, crumbled
- 1 teaspoon curry powder
- ¼ cup skim milk
- 1 teaspoon olive oil
- ¼ teaspoon chili flakes

Directions:

1. Heat olive oil in the skillet.
2. Add crumbled tofu and chili flakes.
3. In the bowl, mix the curry powder and skim milk.
4. Pour the liquid over the crumbled-tofu and mix well.
5. Cook tofu scramble for 3 minutes over med-high heat.

Per serving: 100 calories, 11g protein, 3.3g carbs, 6.4g fat, 1.2g fiber, 0mg cholesterol, 25mg sodium, 210mg potassium.

Scallions Omelet

Preparation time: 10 min

Cooking time: 10 min

Servings: 2

Ingredients:

- 1 oz scallions, chopped
- 2 eggs, beaten
- 1 tablespoon low-fat sour cream
- ¼ teaspoon ground black pepper
- 1 teaspoon olive oil

Directions:

1. Heat olive oil in the skillet.
2. Then, in the mixing bowl combine all remaining ingredients.
3. Pour the egg-mix into the hot skillet, flatten well and cook for 7 minutes over medium-low heat.
4. The omelet is cooked when it is nicely browned.

Per serving: 10 calories, 7g protein, 1.8g carbs, 8g fat, 0.4g fiber, 166mg cholesterol, 67mg sodium, 110mg potassium.

Breakfast Almond Smoothie

Preparation time: 5 min

Cooking time: 2 min

Servings: 3

Ingredients:

- ½ cup almonds, chopped
- 1 cup low-fat milk
- 1 banana, peeled, chopped

Directions:

1. Put all ingredients in the mix and blend until smooth.
2. Pour the smoothie into the serving jar.

Per serving: 164 calories, 5.5g protein, 16.4g carbs, 8.8g fat, 3g fiber, 4mg cholesterol, 36mg sodium, 379mg potassium.

Fruits and Rice Pudding

Preparation time: 10 min

Cooking time: 10 min

Servings: 3

Ingredients:

- ½ cup long-grain rice
- 1 ½ cup low-fat milk
- 1 teaspoon vanilla extract
- 2 oz apricots, chopped

Directions:

1. Pour milk and add rice to the saucepan.
2. Close the lid and cook the rice over medium-high heat for 10 minutes.
3. After, add vanilla extract and stir the rice well.
4. Transfer the pudding to the bowls and serve with apricots.

Per serving: 170 calories, 5.4g protein, 32.9g carbs, 0.3g fat, 0.8g fiber, 2mg cholesterol, 67mg sodium, 276mg potassium.

Blueberry Date Muffins

Preparation Time: 15 min

Cooking Time: 24 min

Servings: 10

Ingredients:

- 1 teaspoon baking soda
- ¼ teaspoon kosher or sea salt
- ½ cup old-fashioned rolled oats
- 1 teaspoon baking powder
- ¼ teaspoon ground cinnamon
- ¼ cup oil
- 1¼ cups whole-wheat flour
- 1 teaspoon pure vanilla extract

- ¼ cup dark brown sugar
- 2 large eggs
- 2/3 cup milk
- 8 pitted Medjool dates, chopped
- 1 cup frozen or fresh blueberries

Directions:

1. Preheat the oven to 350°F. Prep 12-cup muffin tin with muffin liners.
2. Mix salt, oats, baking powder, cinnamon baking soda, and flour.
3. In a separate bowl, rinse oil and brown sugar until fluffy. Mix in the vanilla extract and milk until combined. Mix eggs together until well beaten.
4. Stir in the flour mixture to the wet ingredients and stir until combined, then gently fold in the blueberries and dates.
5. Spoon batter evenly into each muffin mold, filling almost to the top. Bake for 25 mins. Set aside before removing from the muffin pan.
6. Store cooled muffins in sealed plastic bags.

Per serving: 180 Calories, 6g Total Fat, 172mg Sodium, 186mg Potassium, 30g Total Carbs, 4g Protein

Broccoli Cheese Egg Muffins

Preparation Time: 15 min

Cooking Time: 30 min

Servings: 4

Ingredients:

- 1 tablespoon olive oil
- 1 small head of broccoli, chopped into bite-size florets (about 4 cups)
- 8 large eggs
- ¼ cup nonfat milk
- 1 teaspoon onion powder
- 1 teaspoon garlic powder
- ¼ teaspoon kosher or sea salt
- ½ teaspoon ground black pepper
- ½ teaspoon dried mustard powder
- 1 cup shredded Cheddar cheese, divided
- Cooking spray

Directions:

1. Preheat the oven to 350°F.
2. Cook the olive oil in a medium skillet over medium heat. Add the broccoli and sauté for 4 to 5 minutes, until soft.
3. In a big mixing bowl, scourge eggs, salt, milk, garlic powder, onion powder, mustard powder and black pepper. Add the sautéed broccoli and half of the Cheddar cheese.
4. Brush a 10-cup muffin mold with cooking spray. Evenly distribute egg mixture into each cup. Sprinkle with the remaining Cheddar cheese. Bake for 22 to 24 mins until the eggs are set.
5. Let the muffins slightly cool before removing them from the tin.
6. Place the egg muffins in microwaveable airtight containers and refrigerate for up to 5 days or freeze for 2 months. Heat it again in the microwave for 1or 2 minutes on high, until heated through.

Per serving: 316 Calories, 23g Total Fat, 496mg Sodium, 323mg Potassium, 7g Total Carbs, 21g Protein

Greek Breakfast Scramble

Preparation Time: 10 min

Cooking Time: 10 min

Servings: 4

Ingredients:

- 1 tablespoon olive oil
- 1-pint grape or cherry tomatoes, quartered
- 2 cups chopped kale
- 2 garlic cloves, peeled and minced
- 8 large eggs
- ¼ teaspoon kosher or sea salt
- ¼ teaspoon ground black pepper ¼ cup crumbled feta
- ¼ cup flat-leaf Italian parsley, chopped

Directions:

1. Cook olive oil in a large nonstick skillet over medium heat. Add the tomatoes and kale. Sauté for 2 to 3 mins, until the kale and tomatoes are slightly soft. Stir in the garlic. Reduce the skillet heat to low.
2. In a medium bowl, scourge eggs, salt, and black pepper. Stir in the egg mixture into the skillet, slowly folding the eggs until fluffy and scrambled. Remove from heat and add feta and parsley.

Per serving: 222 Calories, 15g Total Fat, 383mg Sodium, 195mg Potassium, 7g Total Carbs, 15g Protein

Bean Frittata

Preparation time: 5 min

Cooking time: 12 min

Servings: 4

Ingredients:

- 4 eggs, beaten
- ½ cup red kidney beans, canned
- ½ onion, diced
- 1 tablespoon margarine
- 1 teaspoon dried dill

Directions:

1. Toss the margarine in the skillet. Add onion and sauté it for 4 minutes or until it is soft.
2. Add red kidney beans and dried dill. Mix the mixture up.
3. Combine the eggs over it and close the lid.
4. Cook the frittata on med-low heat for 7 mins or until it is set or bake it in the oven at 390°F for 5 mins.

Per serving: 170 calories, 10g protein, 15.9g carbs, 7.5g fat, 3.8g fiber, 164mg cholesterol, 99mg sodium, 401mg potassium.

Peach Pancakes

Preparation time: 10 min

Cooking time: 10 min

Servings: 6

Ingredients:

- 1 cup whole-wheat flour
- 1 egg, beaten
- 1 teaspoon vanilla extract
- 2 peaches, chopped
- 1 tablespoon margarine
- ½ teaspoon baking powder
- 1 teaspoon apple cider vinegar
- ¼ cup skim milk

Directions:

1. Make the pancake batter: in a bowl, mix up eggs, vanilla extract, whole-wheat flour,

baking powder, apple cider vinegar, and skim milk.
2. Then melt the margarine in the skillet.
3. Pour the prepared batter into the skillet with the help of the ladle and flatten in the shape of the pancake.
4. Cook the pancakes for 2 mins from each side over medium-low heat.
5. Garnish the cooked pancakes with the peaches.

Per serving: 130 calories, 3.8g protein, 21.5g carbs, 3g fat, 1.3g fiber, 27mg cholesterol, 39mg sodium, 188mg potassium.

Breakfast Splits

Preparation time: 15 min

Cooking time: 0 min

Servings: 2

Ingredients:

- 2 bananas, peeled
- 4 tablespoons granola
- 2 tablespoons low-fat yogurt
- ½ teaspoon ground cinnamon
- 1 strawberry, chopped

Directions:

1. In the mixing bowl, mix up strawberries, yogurt and ground cinnamon.
2. Then make lengthwise cuts in the bananas and fill them with the yogurt mass.
3. Top the fruits with granola.

Per serving: 158 calories, 6.8g protein, 45.2g carbs, 8g fat, 6.3g fiber, 1mg cholesterol, 20mg sodium, 635mg potassium.

Banana Pancakes

Preparation time: 10 min

Cooking time: 15 min

Servings: 5

Ingredients:

- 2 bananas, mashed
- ½ cup 1% milk
- 1 ½ cup whole-grain flour
- 1 teaspoon liquid honey
- 1 teaspoon vanilla extract
- 1 teaspoon baking powder
- 1 tablespoon lemon juice
- 1 tablespoon olive oil

Directions:

1. Mix up mashed bananas and milk.
2. Then add liquid honey, flour, vanilla extract, baking powder, and lemon juice.
3. Combine the mixture until you have a smooth batter.
4. Heat olive oil in the skillet.
5. When the oil is very hot, pour the pancake mixture into the pan and flatten it into pancake shapes.
6. Cook them for 1 minute and then flip on another side. Cook the pancakes for 1 minute more.

Per serving: 207 calories, 6.3g protein, 39.9g carbs, 3.9g fat, 5.7g fiber, 1mg cholesterol, 15mg sodium, 458mg potassium.

Mushroom Thyme Frittata

Preparation Time: 15 min

Cooking Time: 25 min

Servings: 6

Ingredients:

- 12 large eggs
- ½ cup nonfat plain Greek yogurt
- 1 tablespoon balsamic vinegar
- ¾ teaspoon kosher or sea salt
- ¼ teaspoon ground black pepper
- 1½ cups shredded Swiss cheese, divided
- 3 tablespoons olive oil
- 1 large shallot, peeled and thinly sliced
- 2 scallions, thinly sliced
- 2 cups sliced mushrooms
- 2 teaspoons fresh thyme leaves, chopped

Directions:

1. Preheat the oven to 375°F.
2. In a mixing bowl, whisk the eggs, Greek yogurt, balsamic vinegar, salt, and black pepper and half of the shredded Swiss cheese until thoroughly combined.
3. Heat the olive oil in a large oven-safe nonstick skillet over medium heat. Add the shallots, scallions, and mushrooms and sauté for 4 to 5 minutes until the mushrooms are soft. Stir in the thyme.
4. Stir in the egg mixture into the skillet with the mushroom mixture and cook 4 to 5 minutes, until the base begins to set. Top with the remaining shredded cheese and transfer to the oven. Bake for 15 mins, until the egg is set.
5. Remove the frittata from the oven and let it slightly cool, then slice into 6 wedges.

Per serving: 333 Calories, 25g Total Fat, 503mg Sodium, 142mg Potassium, 4g Total Carbs, 22g Protein

---

Roasted Root Vegetable Hash

Preparation Time: 20 min

Cooking Time: 40 min

Servings: 4

Ingredients:

- Cooking spray
- 2 small sweet potatoes, peeled and cubed
- 2 parsnips, peeled and sliced
- 1 red onion, thinly sliced
- 2 tablespoons olive oil
- ½ tablespoon balsamic vinegar
- ¼ teaspoon kosher or sea salt
- ½ teaspoon ground black pepper
- ¼ teaspoon crushed red pepper flakes
- 8 Perfectly Poached Eggs

Directions:

1. Preheat the oven to 400°F. Brush the baking sheet with cooking spray.
2. Place the sweet potatoes, parsnips, and red onion on the greased baking sheet. Pour the olive oil and vinegar (balsamic) and season with salt, black pepper, and crushed red pepper flakes. Toss to coat.
3. Roast for 35 to 40 mins, until vegetables are fork-tender and crispy on the outside.
4. Serve with Perfectly Poached Eggs.
5. Evenly divide the hash and eggs into microwaveable airtight containers. Heat it again in the microwave on high for 1 to 2 minutes.

Per serving: 343 Calories, 17g Total Fat, 306mg Sodium, 602mg Potassium, 33g Total Carbs, 15g Protein

---

Hash Brown Vegetable Breakfast Casserole

Preparation Time: 23 min

Cooking Time: 47 min

Servings: 6

Ingredients:

- 12 large eggs
- 1½ cups plain nonfat Greek yogurt
- 1 teaspoon onion powder
- 1 teaspoon garlic powder
- ½ teaspoon kosher or sea salt
- ½ teaspoon ground black pepper
- ¼ teaspoon crushed red pepper flakes
- 3 cups shredded hash brown potatoes
- 2 cups baby spinach leaves, roughly chopped
- 1 red bell pepper, seeded and diced
- 1½ cups shredded sharp Cheddar cheese, divided

Directions:

1. Preheat the oven to 375°F. Brush a 9-by-13-inch baking dish with cooking spray.
2. Using a big mixing bowl, whisk the eggs, Greek yogurt, onion powder, garlic powder, salt, red pepper flakes and black pepper until beaten and combined. Fold in the potatoes, spinach, and red bell pepper and half the sharp Cheddar cheese. Stir in the mixture into the prepared baking dish. Sprinkle the remaining shredded cheese evenly over the top.
3. Bake for 35 to 45 mins, until the egg is set. Remove and allow to slightly cool, then slice into 6 pieces.

Per serving: 363 Calories, 19g Total Fat, 568mg Sodium, 169mg Potassium, 21g Total Carbs, 26g Protein

---

Sweet Potato Pancakes with Maple Yogurt

Preparation Time: 15 min

Cooking Time: 20 min

Servings: 6

Ingredients:

- 2 cups whole-wheat flour
- 1 tablespoon baking powder
- 1½ teaspoons pumpkin pie spice
- ½ teaspoon kosher or sea salt
- 2 tablespoons dark brown sugar
- 4 tablespoons canola oil
- 2 large eggs
- 1 cup sweet potato purée or cooked mashed sweet potato
- 1½ cups nonfat milk
- 1 teaspoon pure vanilla extract Cooking spray
- 1½ cups plain nonfat Greek yogurt
- ½ teaspoon maple extract or 1 tablespoon pure maple syrup

Directions:

1. Scourge flour, baking powder, pumpkin pie spice, and salt until combined.
2. Using a separate mixing bowl, with a hand mixer set on medium speed, beat the brown sugar and canola oil

together until fluffy. While the hand mixer is still beating, add one egg at a time until thoroughly combined. Add the sweet potato purée then the milk and vanilla extract until well blended. With a hand mixer to low speed and slowly add the dry ingredient mixture until well blended.

3. Heat a wide nonstick skillet over medium heat. Coat the pan with cooking spray. Working in batches, ladle ¼-cup dollops of pancake batter into the pan. Cook for 1 to 2 mins, until bubbles appear on the top, then flip and cook for another 1 to 2 minutes, until set. Repeat with the remaining batter.

4. Scourge Greek yogurt and maple extract or maple syrup until combined. Serve it over the sweet potato pancakes.

Per serving: 355 Calories, 12g Total Fat, 305mg Sodium, 477mg Potassium, 50g Total Carbs, 16g Protein

Whole-Grain Flax Waffles with Strawberry Purée

Preparation Time: 15 min

Cooking Time: 15 min

Serving: 6

Ingredients:

- 1-quart strawberries, hulled and chopped
- 1 cup water
- 2 tablespoons honey
- 2½ teaspoons pure vanilla extract, divided
- 2¼ cups whole-wheat flour
- ¼ cup ground flaxseed
- 2½ teaspoons baking powder
- 1 teaspoon baking soda
- ½ teaspoon kosher or sea salt
- 2 teaspoons ground cinnamon
- 2 tablespoons dark brown sugar
- ¼ cup canola oil
- 3 large eggs
- 1 cup nonfat milk
- Cooking spray

Directions:

1. First, make the strawberry purée: Place the strawberries, water, and honey and ½ teaspoon of vanilla extract in a medium saucepan. Bring to a simmer for 5 to 6 minutes, until the strawberries are soft. Use an immersion blender to purée the strawberries or transfer the mixture to a blender and purée until smooth. 2. To make the waffles: In a medium mixing bowl, whisk the flour, flaxseed, baking powder, baking soda, and salt until combined.

2. Scourge ground cinnamon, brown sugar, and canola oil until well combined. Whisk in one egg at a time until the mixture is fluffy. Add the remaining vanilla extract and milk until incorporated. Slowly whisk the dry ingredients into the wet mixture.

3. Heat a Belgian waffle maker over medium heat. Once hot, coat with the cooking spray. Evenly spoon 2/3 cup batter into the waffle maker. Shut the lid and cook for 1½ to 2 minutes until the waffle is browned on the outside. Repeat with the remaining batter.

4. Serve the waffles with the strawberry purée.

Per serving: 381 Calories, 15g Total Fa,t 459mg Sodium, 452mg Potassium, 12g Protein

Blueberry Waffles

Preparation Time: 5 min

Cooking Time: 15 min

Servings: 8

Ingredients:

- 2 cups whole wheat flour
- 1 tablespoon baking powder
- 1 teaspoon ground cinnamon
- 2 tablespoons sugar
- 2 large eggs
- 3 tablespoons unsalted butter, melted
- 3 tablespoons nonfat plain Greek yogurt
- 1½ cups 1% milk
- 2 teaspoons vanilla extract
- 4 ounces blueberries
- Nonstick cooking spray
- ½ cup maple almond butter

Directions:

1. Preheat waffle iron.
2. Mix flour, baking powder, cinnamon, and sugar.
3. Scourge eggs, melted butter, yogurt, milk, and vanilla. Combine well.
4. Pour in wet ingredients to the dry mix and whisk until well combined. Do not over whisk; it's okay if the mixture has some lumps. Fold in the blueberries.
5. Coat the waffle iron with cooking spray. Put 1/3 cup of the batter onto the iron and cook until the waffles are lightly browned and slightly crisp. Repeat with the rest of the batter.
6. Place 2 waffles in each of 4 storage containers. Store the almond butter in 4 condiment cups. To serve, top each warm waffle with 1 tablespoon of maple almond butter.

Per serving: 647 Calories, 37g Total fat, 67g Carbs, 22g Protein, 296mg Potassium, 156mg Sodium

Apple Pancakes

Preparation Time: 5 min

Cooking Time: 9 min

Serving: 8

Ingredients:

- ¼ cup extra-virgin olive oil, divided
- 1 cup whole wheat flour
- 2 teaspoons baking powder
- 1 teaspoon baking soda
- 1 teaspoon ground cinnamon
- 1 cup 1% milk
- 2 large eggs
- 1 medium Gala apple, diced
- 2 tablespoons maple syrup
- ¼ cup chopped walnuts

Directions:

1. Set aside 1 teaspoon of oil to use for oil a griddle or skillet. Mix the flour, baking powder, baking soda, cinnamon, milk, eggs, apple, and the remaining oil.
2. Heat a pan or skillet over med-high heat and coat with the reserved oil. Working in batches, pour in about ¼ cup of the batter for each pancake. Cook until browned on both sides.
3. Place 4 pancakes into each of 4 medium storage containers and the maple syrup in

4 small containers. To serve, sprinkle each serving with 1 tbspoon of walnuts and drizzle with ½ tablespoon of maple syrup.

Per serving: 378 Calories, 22g Total fat, 39g Carbohydrates, 10g Protein, 334mg Potassium, 65mg Sodium

---

Egg Toasts

Preparation time: 5 min

Cooking time: 5 min

Servings: 3

Ingredients:

- 3 eggs
- 3 whole-grain bread slices
- 1 teaspoon olive oil
- ¼ teaspoon minced garlic
- ¼ teaspoon ground black pepper

Directions:

1. Heat olive oil in the skillet.
2. Mix the eggs inside and cook them for 4 minutes.
3. Then, rub the bread slices with minced garlic.
4. Top the bread with cooked eggs and drizzle with black pepper.

Per serving: 155 calories, 8.6g protein, 13.5g carbs, 7.4g fat, 2.1g fiber, 164mg cholesterol, 182mg sodium, 62mg potassium.

Sweet Yogurt with Figs

Preparation time: 5 min

Cooking time: 0 min

Servings: 1

Ingredients:

- 1/3 cup low-fat yogurt
- 1 teaspoon almond flakes
- 1 fresh fig, chopped
- 1 teaspoon liquid honey
- ¼ teaspoon sesame seeds

Directions:

1. Mix up honey, yogurt and pour the mixture into the serving glass.
2. Top it with sesame seeds, chopped fig and almond flakes.

Per serving: 177 calories, 6.2g protein, 24.4g carbs, 6.8g fat, 3.1g fiber, 5mg cholesterol, 44mg sodium, 283mg potassium.

Very Berry Muesli

Preparation time: 10 min

Servings: 2

Ingredients:

- 1 cup old-fashioned rolled oats (raw)
- 1 cup fruit yogurt
- 1/2 cup 1% milk
- Pinch of salt
- 1/2 cup dried fruit (try raisins, apricots, dates)
- 1/2 cup chopped apple
- 1/2 cup frozen blueberries
- 1/4 cup chopped, toasted walnuts

Directions:

1. Mix the oatmeal, yogurt, milk, and salt in a medium dish.
2. Cover and refrigerate for 6-12 hours.
3. Gently blend and add dried and fresh berries.
4. In little bowls, serve scoops of muesli. Sprinkle with chopped nuts for each meal.
5. Leftovers can be refrigerated within 2-3 hours.

Veggie Quiche Muffins

Preparation time: 30 min

Servings: 12

Ingredients:

- ¾ cup low-fat cheddar cheese, shredded
- 1 cup green onion or onion, chopped
- 1 cup broccoli, chopped
- 1 cup tomatoes, diced
- 2 cups nonfat or 1% milk
- 4 eggs
- 1 cup baking mix (for biscuits or pancakes)
- 1 teaspoon Italian seasoning (or dried leaf basil and oregano)
- ½ teaspoon salt
- ½ teaspoon pepper

Directions:

1. Heat the oven to 375°C. Lightly spray 12 muffin cups or grease them.
2. Sprinkle the muffin cups with cheese, mushrooms, broccoli, and tomatoes.
3. In a cup, place the rest of the ingredients and beat until smooth. In muffin cups, pour egg mixture over remaining ingredients.
4. Bake for 35-40 mins, until golden brown or the knife inserted in the middle, comes out clean. Cool for five minutes.
5. Leftovers should be refrigerated within 2 hours.

Sweet Millet Congee

Preparation time: 35 min

Servings: 8

Ingredients:

- 8 strips of bacon
- 1 cup hulled millet
- 5 cups of water
- 1 cup sweet potato, peeled and diced
- 2 teaspoons ginger, minced (optional)
- 1 teaspoon ground cinnamon
- 2 Tablespoons brown sugar
- 1 medium apple, diced with skin
- ¼ cup honey

Directions:

1. Cook the bacon in a casserole until crispy, over medium-high heat. To extract extra fat, remove it from the pan and blot it with a paper towel. Crumble the bacon strips until cooled, and set aside.
2. Rinse the millet and drain it.
3. Blend the millet, water, sweet potato, ginger, cinnamon, and brown sugar in a deep bath. Put to a boil, reduce heat to low, and simmer until water is absorbed, stirring regularly (about 1 hour).
4. If the millet has been baked, remove the pot from the heat and add apple, honey, and bacon crumbles.
5. Method of slow cooking: Minimize water by 1 cup and cook 2 to 2 1/2 hours on high.

Summer Breakfast Quinoa Bowls

Preparation time: 35 min

Servings: 2

Ingredients:

- 1 small peach, sliced
- 1/3 cup uncooked quinoa, rinsed well
- 2/3 + 3/4 cup low-fat milk
- ½ teaspoon vanilla extract
- 2 teaspoons brown sugar
- 12 raspberries
- 14 blueberries
- 2 teaspoons honey

Directions:

1. Combine the quinoa, 2/3 cup milk, vanilla, and brown sugar in the saucepan.
2. Cook and bring to a boil for five minutes over medium heat. Lower the heat to low and cover up. Cook for 15 to 20 minutes or before the fork fluffs quickly.
3. Meanwhile, the grill pan is heated and sprayed with grease. Grill the peaches for 2 to 3 mins to bring out their sweetness; set aside. In the refrigerator, melt the leftover milk.
4. Divide the cooked quinoa into 2 containers, then add the warmed milk into them. Drizzle each with 1 tsp of honey and finish with peaches, raspberries, and blueberries.

Red Velvet Pancakes with Cream Cheese Topping

Preparation time: 25 min

Servings: 5

Ingredients:

Cream Cheese Topping:

- 2 ounces 1/3 less fat cream cheese
- 3 tablespoons plain fat-free yogurt
- 3 tablespoons honey
- 1 tablespoon fat-free milk

Pancakes:

- ½ cup white whole wheat flour
- ½ cup unbleached all-purpose flour
- 2 ¼ teaspoons baking powder
- ½ tablespoon unsweetened cocoa powder
- ¼ teaspoon salt
- ¼ cup of sugar
- 1 large egg
- 1 cup + 2 tablespoons fat-free milk
- 1 teaspoon vanilla
- ½ teaspoon red paste food coloring

Directions:

1. Mix and set aside the cream cheese topping ingredients.
2. Combine the flour, baking powder, chocolate powder, sugar, and salt in a big bowl.
3. Dissolve the food coloring with the milk in another one; whisk in the egg and vanilla.
4. Until there are no more dry spots, mix the wet and dry ingredients, being careful not to over mix.
5. On a medium-low fire, heat a large nonstick griddle pan. Spray lightly with oil to cover when wet, and spill 1/4 cup of the pancake batter into the pan.
6. Flip the pancakes as soon as the pancake begins to bubble and the edges start to set. Repeat for the batter left.

7. Place 2 pancakes on each plate to eat, then finish with approximately 2,1/2 tablespoons of cream cheese topping.

Vanilla Toasts

Preparation time: 10 min

Cooking time: 5 min

Servings: 3

Ingredients:

- 3 whole-grain bread slices
- 1 teaspoon vanilla extract
- 1 egg, beaten
- 2 tablespoons low-fat sour cream
- 1 tablespoon margarine

Directions:

1. Melt the butter in the skillet.
2. Then, in the bowl, mix up vanilla extract, eggs, and low-fat sour cream.
3. Toss the bread slices in the egg mixture well.
4. After, transfer them in the melted margarine and roast for 2 mins from each side.

Per serving: 160 calories,4.1g protein, 18.7g carbs, 7.9g fat, 2g fiber, 58mg cholesterol, 229mg sodium, 39mg potassium.

Raspberry Yogurt

Preparation time: 5min

Cooking time: 0 min

Servings: 2

Ingredients:

- ½ cup low-fat yogurt
- ½ cup raspberries
- 1 teaspoon almond flakes

Directions:

1. Mix up raspberries, yogurt and transfer them to the serving glasses.
2. Top with almond flakes.

Per serving: 73 calories,3.9g protein, 8.6g carbs, 3.4g fat, 2.6g fiber, 4mg cholesterol, 32mg sodium, 192mg potassium.

Salsa Eggs

Preparation time: 10 min

Cooking time: 10 min

Servings: 4

Ingredients:

- 2 tomatoes, chopped
- 1 chili pepper, chopped
- 2 cucumbers, chopped
- 1 red onion, chopped
- 2 tablespoons parsley, chopped
- 1 tablespoon olive oil
- 1 tablespoon lemon juice
- 4 eggs
- 1 cup water for cooking eggs

Directions:

1. Pour eggs in the water and boil them for 7 mins. Cool the cooked eggs in cold water and peel them.

2. Then, make salsa salad: mix up tomatoes, chili pepper, cucumbers, red onion, parsley, olive oil, and lemon juice.
3. Slice the eggs into the halves and drizzle generously with cooked salsa salad.

Per serving: 144 calories, 7.5g protein, 11.1g carbs, 8.3g fat, 2.2g fiber, 164mg cholesterol, 71mg sodium, 484mg potassium.

Fruit Scones

Preparation time: 10 min

Cooking time: 12 min

Servings: 8

Ingredients:

- 2 cups whole-grain wheat flour
- ½ teaspoon baking powder
- ¼ cup cranberries, dried
- ¼ cup chia seeds
- ¼ cup apricots, chopped
- ¼ cup almonds, chopped
- 1 tablespoon liquid honey
- 1 egg, whisked

Directions:

1. In the bowl, mix all ingredients and work the dough.
2. Cut the dough into 16 pieces (scones)
3. Bake them at 350F for 13 minutes in the lined baking paper tray.
4. Let scones cool well.

Per serving: 158 calories, 6.1g protein, 27.1g carbs, 3.7g fat, 5.5g fiber, 20mg cholesterol, 10mg sodium, 216mg potassium.

Side Dishes

Sautéed Swiss Chard

Preparation time: 5 min

Cooking time: 10 min

Servings: 6

Ingredients:

- 15 oz swiss chard, chopped
- ½ cup of soy milk
- 1 teaspoon chili powder
- 1 tablespoon avocado oil
- 1 teaspoon whole-grain wheat flour
- ¼ onion, diced

Directions:

1. Warm the avocado oil in the skillet and add the onion. Sauté it for 3 minutes.
2. Stir well and add flour and soy milk. Whisk the mixture until smooth.
3. Add Swiss chard and gently mix ingredients again.
4. Close the lid and sauté the side dish for 5 minutes over medium-low heat.

Per serving: 38 calories, 2.1g protein, 5g carbs, 0.9g fat, 1.7g fiber, 0mg cholesterol, 167mg sodium, 317mg potassium.

Asian Style Asparagus

Preparation time: 5 min

Cooking time: 10 min

Servings: 2

Ingredients:

- 8 oz asparagus, chopped
- 1 tablespoon balsamic vinegar
- 1 teaspoon lime zest, grated
- 1 teaspoon sesame seeds
- ¼ teaspoon ground cumin
- 2 tablespoons margarine

Directions:

1. Put 1 tablespoon of margarine in the skillet and add chopped asparagus.
2. Add the lime zest and roast the vegetables for 5 minutes. Stir once in a while.
3. Then, sprinkle the vegetables with ground cumin and add the remaining margarine.
4. Bake the asparagus for 5 mins at 400F in the oven.
5. Then drizzle the cooked vegetables with balsamic vinegar and sesame seeds. Shake the side dish well.

Per serving: 130 calories, 3g protein, 5.2g carbs, 12.3g fat, 2.7g fiber, 0mg cholesterol, 136mg sodium, 254mg potassium.

Aromatic Cauliflower Florets

Preparation time: 7 min

Cooking time: 18 min

Servings: 6

Ingredients:

- 1-pound cauliflower florets
- 1 tablespoon curry powder
- ¼ cup of soy milk
- 1 tablespoon margarine
- ½ teaspoon dried oregano

Directions:

1. Preheat the oven to 375F.

2. Then, melt the margarine in the saucepan.
3. Combine together soy milk and curry powder and whisk the liquid until smooth.
4. After, pour it in the saucepan with the melted margarine and bring to boil.
5. Add cauliflower florets and stir well.
6. Then, close the lid and cook the vegetables for 5 minutes. Transfer the pan to the preheated oven and cook the meal for 10 mins, until the florets are soft.

Per serving: 50calories, 2g protein, 5.4g carbohydrates, 2.3g fat, 2.4g fiber, 0mg cholesterol, 51mg sodium, 260mg potassium.

Brussel Sprouts Mix

Preparation time: 6 min

Cooking time: 15 min

Servings: 2

Ingredients:

- 1 cup Brussel sprouts, sliced
- 1 tablespoon olive oil
- 1 tomato, chopped
- ½ cup fresh parsley, chopped
- 2 oz leek, sliced
- 1 cup vegetable broth
- ½ jalapeno pepper, chopped

Directions:

1. Pour olive oil into the saucepan.
2. Add sliced Brussels sprouts and leek and cook for 5 minutes. Stir the vegetables from time to time.
3. After this, add parsley, chopped tomato, jalapeno, and vegetable broth.
4. Close the lid and cook at medium-high heat for 10 min. Mesh the vegetables during cooking to avoid burning.

Per serving: 66 calories, 2.6g protein, 5.4g carbs, 4.1g fat, 1.6g fiber, 0mg cholesterol, 204mg sodium, 2451mg potassium.

Braised Baby Carrot

Preparation Time: 5 min

Cooking Time: 22 min

Servings: 2

Ingredients:

- 1 cup baby carrots
- 1 teaspoon dried thyme
- 1 tablespoon olive oil
- ½ cup vegetable stock
- 1 garlic clove, sliced

Directions:

1. Heat olive oil in the saucepan for 30 seconds.
2. Then add sliced garlic and dried thyme. Bring the mixture to a boil and add the baby carrot.
3. Roast the vegetables for 7 minutes over medium heat. Stir them constantly.
4. Then, add vegetable stock and close the lid.
5. Cook the baby carrots for 15 min, until they are tender.

Per serving: 69 calories, 0.6g protein, 5.6g carbs, 4.8g fat, 111mg sodium, 141mg potassium

Acorn Squash with Apples

Preparation Time: 20-25 min

Servings: 2

Ingredients:

- 1 Granny Smith apple
- 2 tablespoon Brown sugar
- 1 Acorn squash, small or about 6 inches in diameter
- 2 teaspoon Margarine - trans-fat-free

Directions:

1. Peel the apple, remove core and slice.
2. Toss the apple and brown sugar. Set aside.
3. Poke a few holes in the squash. Pop it into the microwave for 5 min using the high-power setting.
4. Rotate the squash after three minutes.
5. Put it on the chopping block and slice it in half. Discard the seeds and load the hollowed squash with the apple mixture.
6. Pop the container back into the microwave and continue cooking the apples until they're softened (2 min.).
7. Serve the squash with a portion of margarine.

Per serving: 204 Calories, 40g Carbs, 4g Fat, 2g Protein, 6g Sugar, 6g Fiber, 46mg Sodium

Asparagus with Horseradish Dip

Preparation Time: 15 min

Servings: 16

Ingredients:

- 32/about 2 lb. fresh asparagus spears
- 1 cup Reduced-fat mayonnaise
- ¼ cup Parmesan cheese - grated
- 1 tablespoon Prepared horseradish
- ½ teaspoon Worcestershire sauce

Directions:

1. Trim and place the asparagus in a steamer basket in a large saucepan (over one inch of water).
2. Wait for it to boil by covering. Steam until crisp-tender (2-4 min.).
3. Drain and immediately place it into ice water to chill. Drain it into a colander and pat dry.
4. Combine the rest of the fixings.
5. Serve with asparagus.

Per serving: 2 spears with 1 tbsp. of dip: 63 Calories, 3g Carbs, 5g Fat, 1g Protein, 1g Sugar, 146mg Sodium

Grilled Tomatoes

Preparation Time: 10 min

Cooking Time: 2 min

Servings: 4

Ingredients:

- 4 tomatoes
- ½ teaspoon dried basil
- 1 tablespoon olive oil
- ½ teaspoon dried oregano

Directions:

1. Preheat the grill to 390F.
2. Slice the tomatoes and sprinkle with dried oregano and dried basil.

3. Then, sprinkle the vegetables with olive oil and place them in the preheated grill.
4. Grill the tomatoes for 1 minute from each side.

Per serving: 55 calories, 1.1g protein, 4.9g carbs, 3.8g fat, 6mg sodium, 295mg potassium.

Parsley Celery Root

Preparation Time: 7 min

Cooking Time: 20 min

Servings: 4

Ingredients:

- 2 cups celery root, chopped
- 2 oz fresh parsley, chopped
- 1 tablespoon margarine
- 1 teaspoon olive oil
- 1 teaspoon cumin seeds
- ¼ cup of water

Directions:

1. Mix up olive oil and margarine in the skillet.
2. Add cumin seeds and heat the mixture for 1-2 minutes or until you get the light cumin smell.
3. Then, add chopped celery root and roast it for 8 minutes (for 4 minutes from each side).
4. Then add water and parsley. Close the lid.
5. Cook the vegetables for 8 mins on medium-low heat or until it is tender.

Per serving: 79 calories, 1.7g protein, 8.3g carbs, 4.5g fat, 121mg sodium, 324mg potassium.

Garlic Black Eyed Peas

Preparation Time: 10 min

Cooking Time: 120 min

Servings: 4

Ingredients:

- 2 garlic cloves, diced
- 1/3 cup black eye peace, soaked
- 1 tablespoon scallions, chopped
- 1 tablespoon avocado oil
- 1 teaspoon cayenne pepper
- 2 cups water

Directions:

1. In the skillet mix up garlic, scallions, cayenne pepper, and avocado oil.
2. Roast the mixture for 1 minute.
3. Add black eye peace and water.
4. Then, close the lid and cook the meal over low heat for 2 hours or until the black eye is soft.

Per serving: 25 calories, 1.2g protein, 3.7g carbs, 0.7g fat, 37mg sodium, 31mg potassium

Corn Relish

Preparation Time: 35 min

Cooking Time: 0 min

Servings: 5

Ingredients:

- 1 cup corn kernels, cooked
- ½ cup black beans, cooked
- 1 bell pepper, chopped
- ½ red onion, diced
- 2 tomatoes, chopped
- 1 tablespoon sesame oil
- 2 tablespoons lemon juice

Directions:

1. Combine all ingredients in the big bowl and leave it in the fridge for 30 minutes to marinate.
2. Shake the corn relish well before serving.

Per serving: 150 calories, 6g protein, 22.8g carbs, 3.6g fat, 10mg sodium, 556mg potassium.

Braised Artichokes

Preparation time: 15 min

Cooking time: 35 min

Servings: 4

Ingredients:

- 4 artichokes, trimmed
- 4 garlic cloves, minced
- 4 tablespoons olive oil
- 1 lemon
- 1 cup of water
- 1 teaspoon dried cilantro
- ½ teaspoon dried basil

Directions:

1. Squeeze the juice from the lemon into the saucepan.
2. Add water.
3. Then, in the shallow bowl, mix up garlic, olive oil, dried cilantro, and dried basil.
4. Rub the artichokes with the garlic mixture and place them in the lemon and water.
5. Close lid and cook vegetables for 35 minutes or until tender.
6. Drizzle the cooked artichokes with the lemon and water mixture..

Per serving: 200 calories, 5.7g protein, 19.4g carbs, 14.3g fat, 9.2g fiber, 0mg cholesterol, 155mg sodium, 633mg potassium.

Spiced Eggplant Slices

Preparation time: 10 min

Cooking time: 10 min

Servings: 2

Ingredients:

- 1 chili pepper, minced
- 1 bell pepper, minced
- 1 teaspoon ground cumin
- ¼ teaspoon dried dill
- 2 tablespoons olive oil
- 1 large eggplant, sliced
- ¼ cup of water

Directions:

1. In the bowl, mix up minced chili pepper, ground cumin, and bell pepper.
2. After this, pour olive oil into the skillet.
3. Add the eggplants to the skillet and cook them for 2 minutes from each side.
4. Top every eggplant slice with shredded chili pepper mix and add water.
5. Close the lid and cook the vegetables for 5 mins over medium heat.

Per serving: 197 calories, 3.1g protein, 18.7g carbs, 14.8g fat, 9.1g fiber, 0mg cholesterol, 9mg sodium, 664mg potassium.

Lentil Sauté

Preparation time: 5 min

Cooking time: 40 min

Servings: 4

Ingredients:

- ½ cup lentils
- 1 cup spinach
- 4 cups of water
- 1 teaspoon cayenne pepper
- ½ teaspoon ground coriander
- 1 garlic clove
- 1 tomato, chopped

Directions:

1. Mix all ingredients in the saucepan and stir them gently.
2. Close the lid and cook the sauté for 40 minutes on medium-high heat.

Per serving: 90 calories, 6.6g protein, 15.8g carbs, 0.4g fat, 7.8g fiber, 0mg cholesterol, 16mg sodium, 322mg potassium.

Italian Style Zucchini Coins

Preparation time: 10 min

Cooking time: 5 min

Servings: 2

Ingredients:

- 2 zucchinis, sliced
- 1 tablespoon Italian seasonings
- 2 tablespoons olive oil
- ¼ teaspoon garlic powder

Directions:

1. Dip the zucchini slices with Italian seasonings and garlic powder.
2. Then heat olive oil in the skillet.
3. Place the zucchini rings in the saucepan in one layer and cook them for 1 min from each side or until they are gently brown.
4. Dry the zucchini with the help of a paper towel.

Per serving: 170 calories, 2.5g protein, 7.6g carbs, 16.4g fat, 2.2g fiber, 5mg cholesterol, 22mg sodium, 521mg potassium.

Brussels Sprouts with Shallots & Lemon

Preparation Time: 25 min

Servings: 4

Ingredients:

- 3 teaspoon Olive oil - divided
- 3 tbsp Shallots, sliced thin
- ¼ teaspoon Salt - divided
- 1 lb. Brussels sprouts
- ½ Vegetable stock/broth - no-salt
- ¼ Lemon zest - finely grated
- 1 tablespoon Lemon juice - fresh squeezed
- ¼ teaspoon Black pepper

Directions:

1. Warm a large, nonstick skillet to heat two teaspoons of oil using the medium temperature setting. Add and sauté the shallots until softened and lightly golden (6 min.)
2. Stir in salt (⅛ tsp.). Transfer to a bowl and set aside.
3. In the same pan, warm the rest of the oil (1 tsp) over medium heat.
4. Cut the Brussels sprouts into quarters. Add them to the pan to sauté them for three to four minutes.
5. Add the vegetable stock and wait for it to heat. Simmer with the top of the pan until the Brussels sprouts are tender or about five to six minutes.
6. Scoop the shallots into the pan, mix in the lemon zest and juice, pepper, and the rest of the salt (⅛ tsp.).
7. Enjoy them right away.

Per serving: 104 Calories, 12 g Carbs, 4g Fat, 5g Protein, 3g Sugar, 5g Fiber, 191mg Sodium

Chili-Lime Grilled Pineapple

Preparation Time: 15 min

Servings: 6

Ingredients:

- 1 Fresh pineapple
- 1 tablespoon Honey/agave nectar
- 3 tablespoon Brown sugar
- 1 tablespoon Lime juice
- 1 tablespoon Olive oil
- ½ teaspoon Salt
- 1 ½ Chili powder

Directions:

1. Peel pineapple, removing any eyes from fruit. Cut lengthwise into six wedges; remove the core.
2. Whisk the rest of the fixings until blended. Brush pineapple with half of the glaze; reserve the remaining mixture for basting.
3. Grill the pineapple with the lid on using the medium temperature setting. You can also choose to broil it until it's lightly browned (2-4 min. per side), occasionally basting with the reserved glaze.

Per serving: 97 Calories, 20g Carbs, 2g Fat, 1g Protein, 17 g Sugar, 1g Fiber, 35mg Sodium

Light Wild Rice

Preparation time: 10 min

Cooking time: 45 min

Servings: 6

Ingredients:

- 1 cup wild rice
- 3 cups of water
- 1 teaspoon dried dill
- 1 teaspoon dried cilantro
- 1 teaspoon ground paprika
- 1 tablespoon olive oil

Directions:

1. Combine wild rice and olive oil in the saucepan and roast the ingredients for 1 minute.
2. Add all the ingredients and close the lid.
3. Cook the rice on low-medium heat for 45 mins or until it will soak all liquid.

Per serving: 127 calories, 4g protein, 20.3g carbs, 2.7g fat, 1.8g fiber, 0mg cholesterol, 6mg sodium, 129mg potassium.

Mashed Potato with Avocado

Preparation time: 15 min

Cooking time: 10 min

Servings: 4

Ingredients:

- 3 potatoes, peeled, chopped
- 1 avocado, peeled, chopped
- 1 tablespoon margarine
- 1 tablespoon fresh dill, chopped
- 1 cup of water
- ¼ cup of soy milk

Directions:

1. Pour potatoes in the water and boil them until soft.
2. Then transfer the cooked potatoes to the bowl, add avocado and mash the mixture.
3. Add dill, margarine, and soy milk.
4. Mix the mashed potatoes until they are the smooth consistency of flour.

Per serving: 238 calories, 4.3g protein, 30.9g carbs, 13.1g fat, 7.4g fiber, 0mg cholesterol, 57mg sodium, 940mg potassium.

Baked Herbed Carrot

Preparation time: 5 min

Cooking time: 20 min

Servings: 3

Ingredients:

- 2 carrots, peeled
- 1 tablespoon avocado oil
- 1 teaspoon five spices powder
- 2 tablespoons water

Directions:

1. Rub five spices powder with the carrots and sprinkle with avocado oil.
2. Then transfer the vegetables to the tray and sprinkle with water.
3. Bake the carrots for 22 minutes at 375°F or until they are tender.
4. Cut the carrot into pieces.

Per serving: 35 calories, 1g protein, 4.8g carbs, 0.6g fat, 2.3g fiber, 0mg cholesterol, 28mg sodium, 145mg potassium.

Grilled Pineapple Rings

Preparation time: 10 min

Cooking time: 3 min

Servings: 6

Ingredients:

- 1-pound pineapple, peeled
- 1 teaspoon honey
- 1 teaspoon olive oil

Directions:

1. Slice pineapple into rings and put them in the plastic bag.
2. Then, add all remaining ingredients and shake the pineapple rings well.
3. After this, preheat the grill to 400F.
4. After, put the pineapple rings in the grill and roast them for 2 min from each side.

Per serving: 58 calories, 0.4g protein, 10.9g carbs, 0.9g fat, 1.1g fiber, 0mg cholesterol, 1mg sodium, 83mg potassium.

Chickpea Stew

Preparation time: 5 min

Cooking time: 55 min

Servings: 5

Ingredients:

- 1 cup chickpea, soaked
- 1 onion, diced
- 1 tablespoon margarine
- 1 cup spinach, chopped
- 1 teaspoon tomato paste
- 3 cups of water

Directions:

1. Mix all ingredients in the saucepan and close the lid.
2. Cook the stew for 1 hour on medium-high heat.

Per serving: 170 calories, 8.2g protein, 26.8g carbs, 4.7g fat, 7.6g fiber, 0mg cholesterol, 47mg sodium, 429mg potassium.

Quinoa Bowl

Preparation time: 7 min

Cooking time: 7 min

Servings: 5

Ingredients:

- 1 cup quinoa
- 2 cups of water
- 1 avocado, sliced
- 1 teaspoon cayenne pepper
- 1 tablespoon margarine

Directions:

1. Pour water into the saucepan.
2. Then, add quinoa and cook it for 7 minutes.
3. Then add margarine and cayenne pepper. Stir the quinoa well.
4. After, transfer it to the serving dish and top with sliced avocado.

Per serving: 219 calories, 5.6g protein, 25.5g carbs, 12.2g fat, 5.2g fiber, 0mg cholesterol, 34mg sodium, 396mg potassium.

Sautéed Celery Stalk

Preparation time: 8 min

Cooking time: 15 min

Servings: 2

Ingredients:

- 2 cups celery stalk, chopped
- 1 tablespoon margarine
- 1/3 cup low-fat yogurt
- 1 teaspoon Italian seasonings

Directions:

1. Dissolve the margarine in the skillet and add the celery stalk. Toast it for 5 minutes.
2. Then add Italia seasonings and yogurt. Stir the vegetables and close the lid.
3. Sautèe the celery stalk for 10 mins on low-medium heat.

Per serving: 113 calories, 3.1g protein, 6.2g carbs, 7.1g fat, 1.6g fiber, 4mg cholesterol, 177mg sodium, 362mg potassium.

Asparagus in Sauce

Preparation time: 10 min

Cooking time: 20 min

Servings: 4

Ingredients:

- 1-pound asparagus, chopped
- 2 tablespoons garlic sauce
- 1 tablespoon margarine, melted

Directions:

1. Put the asparagus in the pan and sprinkle with melted margarine and garlic sauce.
2. Cook the vegetables at 400°F for 20 minutes.

Per serving: 48 calories, 2.6g protein, 4.9g carbs, 3g fat, 2.4g fiber, 0mg cholesterol, 50mg sodium, 231mg potassium

Thyme Potatoes

Preparation time: 10 min

Cooking time: 35 min

Servings: 8

Ingredients:

- 8 potatoes, halved
- 2 tablespoons olive oil
- ½ teaspoon garlic powder
- 1 teaspoon dried thyme

Directions:

1. Rub the garlic powder with the potatoes and thyme.
2. After, brush the potatoes with olive oil and transfer in the baking pan,
3. Bake the potatoes at 375°F for 40 minutes.

Per serving: 175 calories, 3.6g protein, 33.7g carbs, 3.7g fat, 5.2g fiber, 0mg cholesterol, 13mg sodium, 870mg potassium.

Sesame Seeds Brussel Sprouts

Preparation time: 10 min

Cooking time: 20 min

Servings: 6

Ingredients:

- 2-pounds Brussels sprouts halved
- 1 tablespoon sesame oil
- 2 teaspoons apple cider vinegar
- 2 teaspoons chili sauce
- 1 tablespoon sesame seeds

Directions:

1. Put the Brussel sprouts in the baking saucepan.
2. Drizzle them with sesame oil, apple cider vinegar, and chili sauce.
3. Bake the vegetables at 400°F for 22 minutes.
4. Top the cooked vegetables with sesame seeds.

Per serving: 89 calories, 5.4g protein, 14.2g carbs, 3.6g fat, 5.9g fiber, 0mg cholesterol, 80mg sodium, 598mg potassium.

Potato Pan

Preparation time: 10 min

Cooking time: 50 min

Servings: 8

Ingredients:

- 1-pound potatoes, roughly chopped
- 2 tablespoons olive oil
- 1 white onion, chopped
- ½ cup low-fat milk
- 1 tablespoon thyme, chopped
- ½ cup low-fat parmesan, grated

Directions:

1. Heat a skillet pan with the oil over medium heat, add the onion and sauté it for 5 minutes.
2. Then, add the potatoes and roast them for 5 minutes more.
3. Add all ingredients and cook over medium heat for 45 minutes more.

Per serving: 97 calories, 2.9g protein, 11.3g carbs, 5g fat, 1.8g fiber, 6mg cholesterol, 106mg sodium, 284mg potassium.

Cauliflower Bake

Preparation time: 10 min

Cooking time: 30 min

Servings: 4

Ingredients:

- 2 tablespoons chili sauce
- 3 garlic cloves, minced
- 1 cauliflower head, florets separated
- 1 teaspoon margarine
- ½ cup low-fat milk

Directions:

1. Mix up all ingredients in the baking tray.
2. Cook the meal at 400F for 30 minutes.

Per serving: 40 calories, 2.5g protein, 5.9g carbs, 1.4g fat, 1.7g fiber, 2mg cholesterol, 235mg sodium, 266mg potassium.

Parsley Broccoli

Preparation time: 10 min

Cooking time: 30 min

Servings: 4

Ingredients:

- 2 tablespoons olive oil
- 1-pound broccoli florets
- 1 tablespoon lime juice
- 3 tablespoons parsley, chopped

Directions:

1. Line the baking pan with baking paper.
2. After, put the broccoli inside and sprinkle the vegetables with lime juice, olive oil, and parsley.
3. Cover the broccoli with foil.
4. Bake the meal at 400°F for 30 minutes.

Per serving: 101 calories, 3.3g protein, 8.2g carbs, 7.4g fat, 3.1g fiber, 0mg cholesterol, 40mg sodium, 380mg potassium.

Tomato Brussel Sprouts

Preparation time: 10 min

Cooking time: 25 min

Servings: 4

Ingredients:

- 1 tablespoon olive oil
- 1-pound Brussels sprouts, trimmed and halved
- 1 tablespoon tomato sauce

Directions:

1. In a baking dish, combine the sprouts with the oil and tomato sauce.
2. Bake the vegetables at 400F for 25 minutes.

Per serving: 80 calories, 3.9g protein, 10.5g carbs, 3.9g fat, 4.3g fiber, 0mg cholesterol, 48mg sodium, 453mg potassium.

Soups

Summer Berry Soup

Preparation time: 10 min

Cooking time: 10 min

Servings: 2

Ingredients:

- ½ cup apple juice
- ¼ cup strawberries
- ¼ cup raspberries
- ¼ cup blackberries
- ¼ cup blueberries
- 1 teaspoon potato starch
- ¼ teaspoon ground cinnamon

Directions:

1. Pour apple juice into the saucepan.
2. Add ground cinnamon and all berries. Close the lid and bring to boil.
3. Pour 3 tablespoons of apple juice mixture into the glass, add potato starch and whisk it until smooth.
4. Then pour the starch mixture into the berry soup and stir until the soup is thickened.
5. Close the lid and let the soup to rest for 10 mins.

Per serving: 66 calories, 0.8g protein, 17.3g carbs, 0.4g fat, 3g fiber, 0mg cholesterol, 3mg sodium, 158mg potassium.

Green Beans Soup

Preparation time: 5 min

Cooking time: 40 min

Servings: 4

Ingredients:

- ½ onion, diced
- 1/3 cup green beans, soaked
- 3 cups of water
- ½ sweet pepper, chopped
- 2 potatoes, chopped
- 1 tablespoon fresh cilantro, chopped
- 1 teaspoon chili flakes

Directions:

1. Combine all ingredients in the saucepan and close the lid.
2. Cook the soup on low-medium heat for 40 minutes, until all ingredients are soft.

Per serving: 80 calories, 2.3g protein, 19.8g carbs, 0.2g fat, 3.4g fiber, 0mg cholesterol, 13mg sodium, 505mg potassium.

Turkey Soup

Preparation time: 10 min

Cooking time: 25 min

Servings: 3

Ingredients:

- 1 potato, diced
- 1 cup ground turkey
- 1 teaspoon cayenne pepper
- 1 onion, diced
- 1 tablespoon olive oil
- ¼ carrot, diced
- 2 cups of water

Directions:

1. Heat olive oil in the saucepan and add diced onion and carrot.

2. Cook the vegetables for 3 mins.
3. Then stir them well and add cayenne pepper and ground turkey.
4. After, add diced potato and stir the ingredients well. Cook them for 2 minutes more.
5. Then add water. Check if you put all the ingredients.
6. Close the lid and cook for 22 minutes.

Per serving: 310 calories, 31.8g protein, 14.2g carbs, 16.9g fat, 2.3g fiber, 112mg cholesterol, 131mg sodium, 619mg potassium.

Beef Soup

Preparation time: 7 min

Cooking time: 45 min

Servings: 4

Ingredients:

- 1-pound beef sirloin, chopped
- 4 oz leek, chopped
- 1 tablespoon margarine
- 1 teaspoon chili powder
- 1 potato, chopped
- 3 cups of water

Directions:

1. Mix margarine in the saucepan and melt it.
2. Then, add chopped beef sirloin, leek and chili powder. Cook the ingredients for 4 mins (2 mins per side).
3. After this, add chopped potato and water. Close the lid.
4. Cook for 40 minutes on medium heat.

Per serving: 280 calories, 35.8g protein, 11.8g carbs, 10.2g fat, 1.7g fiber, 101mg cholesterol, 128mg sodium, 702mg potassium.

Cream of Wild Rice Soup

Preparation Time: 40-45 min.

Servings: 4

Ingredients:

- ½ tablespoon Canola oil
- 1 ½ cup Yellow onion
- 1 cup Carrot
- 2 Cloves of garlic
- 1 cup Celery
- 1 ½ cup Kale
- 1 tablespoon Minced parsley
- 2 cups Low-sodium vegetable stock
- 1 teaspoon Fennel seeds - crushed
- 1 cup Unsalted prepared white beans, or ½ of a 15.5 can White beans
- 2 cups 1 % milk
- ½ cup Wild rice - cooked
- 1 teaspoon Black pepper

Directions:

1. Prep a soup pot over a medium temperature setting, add canola oil to get hot.
2. Rinse and drain the beans.
3. Dice/chop and sauté the carrot, celery, garlic, and onions until lightly browned.
4. Chop and fold in the kale, stock, parsley, and other spices. Wait for it to boil.
5. Use a blender to puree the beans with milk. Mix the bean mixture into the soup. Simmer and add rice (½ hour).
6. Serve in heated bowls.

Per serving: 236 Calories, 38g Carbs, 4g Fat, 12g Protein, 12g Sugar, 7g Fiber, 180 g Sodium

---

Curried Cream of Tomato Soup with Apples

Preparation Time: 45 min.

Servings: 8

Ingredients:

- 2 tablespoon Olive oil (2 tbsp.)
- 1 teaspoon Garlic (1 tsp.)
- 1 ½ cups Onion
- 1 cup Celery
- 1 tablespoon Curry powder
- 3 cups Canned tomatoes No-salt-added - drained
- ½ teaspoon Thyme
- 1 Bay leaf
- A pinch Ground black pepper
- 1 cup Long-grain brown rice
- 6 cups Vegetable/chicken broth – low sodium
- 1 cup Milk - Fat-free
- 1 ½ cups Apple cubes

Directions:

1. Warm oil using the medium-temperature setting in a soup pot.
2. Finely chop and add the garlic, celery, and onion. Sauté them until tender (4 min.). Mix in the curry powder and simmer for a minute.
3. Stir in the tomatoes, thyme, bay leaf, rice, and black pepper while heating it.
4. Mix in the broth and wait for it to begin boiling. Cook it for about ½ hour. The rice should be tender. Trash the bay leaf.
5. Dump the soup into a food processor. Close the lid and puree it until it's creamy smooth.
6. Empty the soup back into the pot. Fold2 in the apple cubes and milk, stirring until it's thoroughly heated.
7. Promptly serve the soup in warmed bowls while piping hot.

Per serving: 205 Calories, 32 g Carbs, 5g Fats, 3g Fiber, 89mg Sodium, 8g Protein

---

Potato Fennel Soup

Preparation Time: 35-40 min.

Servings: 8

Ingredients:

- 1 teaspoon Olive oil
- 1 cup Red onion
- 1 large Fennel bulb (about 2 lb.)
- 2 large Russet potatoes
- 1 cup Milk - fat-free milk
- 3 cups Chicken broth - reduced sodium
- 2 teaspoon Lemon juice
- 2 teaspoon Toasted fennel seeds

Directions:

1. Warm the oil using the medium-temperature setting in a large soup pot.
2. Chop and add the onion and fennel. Sauté until softened (5 min.).
3. Peel and slice the potatoes. Toss them into the pot with lemon juice, milk, and chicken broth.
4. Put a lid on the pot and adjust the temperature setting to a simmer until the potatoes are done (15 min.).

5. Put the soup into a food processor to puree until smooth. (Carefully fill - no more than 1/3 full to avoid burns.)
6. Add it back to the pot and heat to serve. Garnish the soup with fennel seeds to serve.

Per serving: 149 Calories, 28g Carbs, 1.5g Fat Content, 6 g Protein, 7 g Sugar, 3g Fiber, 104mg Sodium

---

Tomato Green Bean Soup

Preparation Time: 45 min.

Servings: 9

Ingredients:

- 1 cup Carrots
- 2 teaspoon Butter
- 1 cup Onion
- 6 cups Chicken/vegetable broth - reduced-sodium
- 1 lb Fresh green beans
- 1 clove Garlic
- 3 cups Diced fresh tomatoes
- ¼ cup Freshly minced basil or 1 tablespoon Dried basil
- ½ teaspoon Salt
- ¼ teaspoon Pepper

Directions:

1. Heat a big saucepan to melt the butter. Chop and sauté the carrots with the onions (5 min.).
2. Cut the beans into one-inch pieces and mince the garlic. Stir in the beans, broth, and garlic. Wait for it to boil.
3. Lower the temperature setting and put a top on the saucepan to cook until the veggies are tender (20 min.).
4. Mix in the tomatoes, salt, basil, and pepper.
5. Place a top on the pan and simmer for five more minutes.

Per serving: 58 Calories, 10g Carbs, 1g Fat Content, 5g Sugar, 3g Fiber, 4g Protein, 535mg Sodium

---

Asparagus Cream Soup

Preparation time: 5 min

Cooking time: 30 min

Servings: 2

Ingredients:

- 2 cups low-sodium chicken stock
- 1 cup asparagus, chopped
- 2 tablespoons low-fat sour cream
- 1 teaspoon dried oregano
- 1 garlic clove, diced
- 1 teaspoon olive oil
- 1 cup broccoli, chopped

Directions:

1. Put olive oil into the large skillet and heat it for 1 minute. Then, add garlic and roast it for 1 minute more.
2. Add all ingredients and close the lid.
3. Simmer the soup for 25 minutes.
4. Blend the soup with the immersion blender until smooth.
5. Cook the soup for 3 minutes more.

Per serving: 30 calories, 2.2g protein, 4.1g carbs, 1.8g fat, 1.5g fiber, 1mg cholesterol, 82mg sodium, 149mg potassium.

Pasta Soup

Preparation time: 5 min

Cooking time: 13 min

Servings: 2

Ingredients:

- 2 oz whole-grain pasta
- ½ cup corn kernels
- 1 oz carrot, shredded
- 3 oz celery stalk, chopped
- 2 cups low-sodium chicken stock
- 1 teaspoon ground black pepper

Directions:

1. Bring the chicken to boil and add shredded carrot and celery stalk. Simmer the liquid for 5 minutes.
2. Then, add corn kernels, ground black pepper, and pasta. Stir the soup well.
3. Simmer it on medium heat for 9 minutes.

Per serving: 260 calories, 11.8g protein, 49.6g carbs, 2.6g fat, 9.4g fiber, 0mg cholesterol, 200mg sodium, 273mg potassium.

Black Beans Soup

Preparation time: 8 min

Cooking time: 25 min

Servings: 6

Ingredients:

- 2 cups black beans, cooked
- 1 yellow onion, diced
- ¼ cup sweet pepper, chopped
- 5 cups low-sodium chicken broth
- 1 carrot, shredded
- 1 teaspoon dried oregano
- ½ teaspoon ground cumin
- 1 teaspoon chili flakes
- ½ cup fresh cilantro, chopped
- 1 tablespoon avocado oil

Directions:

1. Put avocado oil in the saucepan and add shredded carrot and onion. Cook the vegetables for 4 minutes. Stir them from time to time.
2. Then, add sweet pepper, black beans, oregano, and all the remaining ingredients.
3. After, close the lid and cook the soup on medium heat for 15 minutes.
4. Then, blend the soup for 1 minute with the help of the immersion blender. The cooked soup should be totally smooth.
5. Cook it for 1 minute more.

Per serving: 241 calories, 16.1g protein, 44.7g carbs, 1.3g fat, 10.8g fiber, 0mg cholesterol, 71mg sodium, 1050mg potassium.

Carrot Soup

Preparation time: 10 min

Cooking time: 35 min

Servings: 3

Ingredients:

- 1 cup carrot, shredded
- 1 teaspoon curry paste
- 1 tablespoon olive oil
- 1 yellow onion, diced
- ½ teaspoon chili flakes
- 1 tablespoon lemon juice
- 2 cups low-sodium chicken broth

Directions:

1. Heat olive oil in the saucepan and add the onion. Cook it until light brown.
2. Add chili flakes, grated carrot, curry paste and chicken broth.
3. Close the lid and cook for 25 mins.
4. Then blend it with the immersion blender until smooth.
5. Add lemon juice and cook for 4 minutes more.

Per serving: 90 calories, 2.2g protein, 8.3g carbs, 5.7g fat, 1.7g fiber, 0mg cholesterol, 74mg sodium, 178mg potassium.

Cucumber and Melon Soup

Preparation time: 25 min

Cooking time: 0 min

Servings: 4

Ingredients:

- 4 cucumbers, chopped
- 9 oz melon, chopped
- ½ cup fresh cilantro, chopped
- 1 teaspoon honey
- 2 tablespoons lemon juice
- ½ teaspoon cayenne pepper

Directions:

1. Pour all ingredients into immersion blender and blend until smooth.
2. Transfer the smooth soup to the serving bowls and refrigerate for 20 minutes before serving.

Per serving: 70 calories, 2.6g protein, 17.9g carbs, 0.6g fat, 2.2g fiber, 0mg cholesterol, 19mg sodium, 638mg potassium.

Green Detox Soup

Preparation time: 10 min

Cooking time: 12 min

Servings: 4

Ingredients:

- 1 onion, diced
- 1 large zucchini, chopped
- 1 teaspoon fresh mint, chopped
- ½ cup celery stalk, chopped
- 1 teaspoon ground paprika
- 1 tablespoon olive oil
- 2 tablespoons lime juice
- 1 cup low-fat yogurt

Directions:

1. Heat olive oil in the saucepan.

2. Then, add diced onion and cook it for 2 minutes. Stir it well.
3. Add zucchini, mint, and celery stalk.
4. Cook the vegetables for 10 minutes. Stir them from time to time.
5. Add lime juice and ground paprika.
6. Blend the vegetables with the immersion blender and remove them from the heat.
7. Add yogurt and stir the soup well.

Per serving: 103 calories, 5protein, 10.8g carbs, 4.5g fat, 1.9g fiber, 4mg cholesterol, 64mg sodium, 448mg potassium.

Low Sodium Vegetable Soup

Preparation time: 10 min

Cooking time: 15 min

Servings: 3

Ingredients:

- 3 cups low-sodium vegetable broth
- ½ cup spinach, chopped
- 1/3 cup broccoli, chopped
- 2 potatoes, chopped
- ¼ cup low-fat yogurt
- 2 oz green beans, cooked
- 1 teaspoon cayenne pepper
- 1 tomato, roughly chopped

Directions:

1. Put vegetable broth into the saucepan and bring it to a boil.
2. Add potatoes, cayenne pepper, and green beans.
3. Bring the ingredients to a boil and heat for 5 minutes.
4. After this, add yogurt, spinach, broccoli, and tomato.
5. Cook the soup for 10 minutes.

Per serving: 122 calories, 6.6g protein, 28.1g carbs, 0.6g fat, 4.8g fiber, 1mg cholesterol, 102mg sodium, 786mg potassium.

Pumpkin Cream Soup

Preparation time: 10 min

Cooking time: 20 min

Servings: 5

Ingredients:

- 1-pound pumpkin, chopped
- 1 teaspoon ground cumin
- ½ cup cauliflower, chopped
- 4 cups of water
- 1 teaspoon ground turmeric
- ½ teaspoon ground nutmeg
- 1 tablespoon fresh dill, chopped
- 1 teaspoon olive oil
- ½ cup skim milk

Directions:

1. Toast the pumpkin with olive oil in the saucepan for 3 minutes.
2. Stir well and add nutmeg, cauliflower, cumin, turmeric and water.
3. Close the lid and cook the soup on low-medium heat until the pumpkin is soft.
4. Blend the mixture until smooth and after add skim milk.
5. Leave the soup from heat for 2 minutes, remove and top with dill.

Per serving: 44 calories, 2.2g protein, 10g carbs, 1.4g fat, 3.1g fiber, 0mg cholesterol, 28mg sodium, 297mg potassium.

Zucchini Noodles Soup

Preparation time: 10 min

Cooking time: 15 min

Servings: 4

Ingredients:

- 2 zucchinis, trimmed
- 4 cups low-sodium chicken stock
- 2 oz fresh parsley, chopped
- ½ teaspoon chili flakes
- 1 oz carrot, shredded
- 1 teaspoon canola oil

Directions:

1. Broil the carrot with canola oil in the saucepan for 5 minutes over medium-low heat.
2. Stir it well and add chicken stock. Bring the mixture to a boil.
3. Then, make the noodles from the zucchini with the help of the spiralizer.
4. Add them to the boiling soup liquid.
5. Add parsley and chili flakes. Bring the soup to a boil and remove it from the heat.
6. Leave for 12 minutes to rest.

Per serving: 33 calories, 2.7g protein, 4.9g carbs, 1.5g fat, 1.7g fiber, 0mg cholesterol, 158mg sodium, 359mg potassium.

Chicken Oatmeal Soup

Preparation time: 10 min

Cooking time: 15 min

Servings: 5

Ingredients:

- 1 cup oats
- 4 cups of water
- 1 oz fresh dill, chopped
- 10 oz chicken fillet, chopped
- 1 teaspoon ground black pepper
- 1 teaspoon potato starch
- ½ carrot, diced

Directions:

1. Put the chicken in the skillet, add water and bring it to a boil. Simmer the chicken for 10
1. minutes.
2. Add oats, dill, ground black pepper and diced carrot.
3. Bring the soup to a boil and add potato starch. Stir it until the soup starts to thicken. Simmer the soup for 5 minutes on low heat.

Per serving: 188 calories, 19.8g protein, 16.1g carbs, 5.5g fat, 2.7g fiber, 50mg cholesterol, 72mg sodium, 411mg potassium.

Celery Cream Soup

Preparation time: 10 min

Cooking time: 25 min

Servings: 4

Ingredients:

- 2 cups celery stalk, chopped
- 1 shallot, chopped
- 1 potato, chopped
- 4 cups low-sodium vegetable stock
- 1 tablespoon margarine
- 1 teaspoon white pepper

Directions:

1. Melt the margarine in the skillet, add shallot and celery stalk. Cook the vegetables for 5 minutes. Stir them occasionally.
2. After this, add vegetable stock and potato.
3. Simmer the soup for 15 minutes.
4. Blend the soup tilly out get the creamy texture and sprinkle with white pepper.
5. Cook it for 5 minutes more.

Per serving: 68 calories, 2.3g protein, 13.3g carbs, 3g fat, 2.9g fiber, 0mg cholesterol, 217mg sodium, 449mg potassium.

Buckwheat Soup

Preparation time: 10 min

Cooking time: 25 min

Servings: 6

Ingredients:

- ½ cup buckwheat
- 1 carrot, chopped
- 1 yellow onion, diced
- 1 tablespoon avocado oil
- 1 tablespoon fresh dill, chopped
- 1-pound chicken breast, chopped
- 1 teaspoon ground black pepper
- 6 cups of water

Directions:

1. Sauté the onion, carrot, and avocado oil in the saucepan for 5 minutes. Stir them from time to time.
2. Then add ground black pepper, buckwheat and chicken breast.
3. Add water and close the lid.
4. Simmer the soup for 20 minutes.
5. Then, add dill and remove the soup from the heat. Leave it for 10 mins to rest.

Per serving: 141 calories, 18.4g protein, 13.5g carbs, 2.7g fat, 2.3g fiber, 48mg cholesterol, 48mg sodium, 433mg potassium.

Parsley Soup

Preparation time: 10 min

Cooking time: 16 min

Servings: 6

Ingredients:

- 2 teaspoons olive oil
- 1 cup carrot, shredded
- 1 cup yellow onion, chopped
- 1 cup celery, chopped
- 6 cups of water
- 1 cup fresh parsley, chopped
- ¼ cup low-fat parmesan, grated

Directions:

1. Heat a pot with the oil over medium-high heat, add onion, carrot, and celery, stir and cook for 7 minutes.
2. Add water and all remaining ingredients.
3. Cook the soup for 8 minutes over medium heat.

Per serving: 40 calories, 1.6g protein, 4.8g carbs, 2.5g fat, 1.5g fiber, 4mg cholesterol, 103mg sodium, 193mg potassium.

Tomato Bean Soup

Preparation time: 10 min

Cooking time: 25 min

Servings: 6

Ingredients:

- 2 teaspoons olive oil
- 2 garlic cloves, minced
- 1-pound green beans, trimmed and halved
- 4 tomatoes, cubed
- 1 teaspoon sweet paprika
- 4 cups of water
- 2 tablespoons dill, chopped

Directions:

1. Heat a pot with the oil over medium-high heat, add the garlic, stir. Sauté the garlic for 5 minutes.
2. Then, add all remaining ingredients and cook the soup for 20 min.

Per serving: 36 calories, 2.4g protein, 9.7g carbs, 1.9g fat, 3.8g fiber, 0mg cholesterol, 16mg sodium, 400mg potassium.

Red Kidney Beans Soup

Preparation time: 10 min

Cooking time: 20 min

Servings: 4

Ingredients:

- 2 teaspoons olive oil
- 1 yellow onion, chopped
- 1 teaspoon cinnamon powder
- 1 cup red kidney beans, cooked
- 3 cups low-sodium chicken broth
- 1 potato, chopped

Directions:

1. Heat a pot with the oil over medium heat, add onion and cinnamon, stir and cook for 6 minutes.
2. Then, add all remaining ingredients and cook them for 14 minutes.
3. Blend the soup until you get a puree texture.

Per serving: 211 calories, 13g protein, 38.9g carbs, 2.9g fat, 8.5g fiber, 0mg cholesterol, 62mg sodium, 844mg potassium.

Pork Soup

Preparation time: 10 min

Cooking time: 25 min

Servings: 4

Ingredients:

- 1 tablespoon avocado oil
- 1 onion, chopped
- 1-pound pork stew meat, cubed
- 4 cups of water
- 1-pound carrots, sliced
- 1 teaspoon tomato paste

Directions:

1. Heat a pot with the oil over medium-high heat, add the onion and pork, and cook the ingredients for 5 minutes.
2. Then, add all remaining ingredients and cook the soup for 20 minutes.

Per serving: 280 calories, 34.5g protein, 14.2g carbs, 11.4g fat, 3.6g fiber, 98mg cholesterol, 155mg sodium, 855mg potassium.

Curry Soup

Preparation time: 10 min

Cooking time: 23 min

Servings: 4

Ingredients:

- 3 tablespoons olive oil
- 8 carrots, peeled and sliced
- 2 teaspoons curry paste
- 4 celery stalks, chopped
- 1 yellow onion, chopped
- 4 cups of water

Directions:

1. Heat a pot with the oil, add onion, celery, and carrots, and stir and cook for 12 minutes.
2. Then add water and curry paste. Mix the soup well and cook it for 15 minutes.
3. When the soup are soft, blend the soup until smooth and simmer it for 3 minute more.

Per serving: 141 calories, 1.6g protein, 15.8g carbs, 12g fat, 3.9g fiber, 0mg cholesterol, 106mg sodium, 477mg potassium.

Yellow Onion Soup

Preparation time: 10 min

Cooking time: 20 min

Servings: 4

Ingredients:

- 1 tablespoon avocado oil
- 1 yellow onion, chopped
- 1 teaspoon ginger, grated
- 1-pound zucchinis, chopped
- 4 cups low-sodium chicken broth
- ½ cup low-fat cream
- 1 teaspoon ground black pepper

Directions:

1. Heat a pot with the oil over medium heat, add the onion and ginger, stir and cook for 5 minutes.
2. Add all remaining ingredients and simmer them over medium heat for 15 minutes.

3. Blend the cooked soup and ladle in the bowls.

Per serving: 61 calories, 4.2g protein, 10.2g carbs, 0.7g fat, 2.2g fiber, 1mg cholesterol, 101mg sodium, 377mg potassium.

Garlic Soup

Preparation time: 10 min

Cooking time: 50 min

Servings: 4

Ingredients:

- 1-pound red kidney beans, cooked
- 8 cups of water
- 1 green bell pepper, chopped
- 1 tomato paste
- 1 yellow onion, chopped
- 1 teaspoon minced garlic
- 1-pound beef sirloin, cubed
- 1 teaspoon garlic powder

Directions:

1. Pour water in a pot and heat up over medium heat.
2. Add all ingredients and close the lid.
3. Simmer the soup for 45 minutes over medium heat.

Per serving: 620 calories, 60.9g protein, 75.8g carbs, 8.4g fat, 18.5g fiber, 101mg cholesterol, 109mg sodium, 2150mg potassium.

Poultry Soup

Preparation time: 10 min

Cooking time: 40 min

Servings: 4

Ingredients:

- 3 oz turkey breast, skinless, boneless, chopped
- 1 tablespoon tomato paste
- 1 tablespoon olive oil
- 2 yellow onions, chopped
- 4 cups of water
- 1 tablespoon oregano, chopped
- ¼ cup carrot, diced

Directions:

1. Heat up a pot with the olive oil over medium-high heat, add the onions and sauté for 5 minutes.
2. Add the turkey and brown it for 5 minutes more.
3. Add the rest of the ingredients, bring to a simmer and cook over medium heat for 30 minutes.

Per serving: 84 calories, 4.6g protein, 8.2g carbs, 4.1g fat, 2.1g fiber, 9mg cholesterol, 236mg sodium, 229mg potassium.

Roasted Tomatoes Soup

Preparation time: 10 min

Cooking time: 20 min

Servings: 4

Ingredients:

- 1 yellow onion, chopped
- 1 carrot, chopped
- 1 tablespoon olive oil
- 15 ounces roasted tomatoes, no-salt-added
- 2 cups of water
- 1 tablespoon tomato paste
- 1 tablespoon basil, dried
- ¼ teaspoon oregano, dried
- 1 teaspoon chili powder

Directions:

1. Heat a pot with the oil over medium heat, add onion, stir and cook for 5 minutes.
2. Add all remaining ingredients and simmer them for 15 minutes.
3. Then blend the soup until you get the creamy texture.

Per serving: 78 calories, 1.5g protein, 9.4g carbs, 3.7g fat, 2.2g fiber, 0mg cholesterol, 38mg sodium, 147mg potassium.

Yogurt Soup

Preparation time: 10 min

Cooking time: 20 min

Servings: 4

Ingredients:

- 3 garlic cloves, minced
- 1 onion, chopped
- 3 carrots, chopped
- 1 tablespoon olive oil
- 2 cups tomatillos, chopped
- 2 cups low-sodium chicken broth
- ½ cup low-fat yogurt
- 1 teaspoon white pepper

Directions:

1. Heat a pot with the oil over medium heat, add the onion and the garlic and sauté for 5 minutes.
2. Add all the remaining ingredients and cook the soup for 15 minutes more.

Per serving: 152 calories, 18.4g protein, 13.5g carbs, 2.7g fat, 2.3g fiber, 48mg cholesterol, 48mg sodium, 433mg potassium.

Salads

Salad Skewers

Preparation time: 10 min

Cooking time: 0 min

Servings: 4

Ingredients:

- 2 cucumbers
- 2 cups cherry tomatoes
- ½ teaspoon lemon juice
- 1 teaspoon olive oil

Directions:

1. Cut the cucumbers into medium cubes.
2. Then string the cherry tomatoes and cucumber cubes into skewers one by one.
3. Then drizzle the salad skewers with lemon juice and olive oil.

Per serving: 40 calories, 1.8g protein, 9g carbs, 1.5g fat, 1.8g fiber, 0mg cholesterol, 8mg sodium, 435mg potassium.

Asian Style Cobb Salad

Preparation time: 10 min

Cooking time: 0 min

Servings: 4

Ingredients:

- 2 cup lettuce, chopped
- 1 cup tangerines, peeled
- 1 cup carrot, grated
- 3 oz scallions, chopped
- 1 avocado, sliced
- 3 tablespoons balsamic vinegar
- 1 tablespoon sesame seeds
- 1 tablespoon lemon zest, grated
- 1 tablespoon avocado oil

Directions:

1. Make the salad dressing: mix balsamic vinegar, sesame seeds, lemon zest, and avocado oil.
2. Pour all remaining ingredients in the bowl and sprinkle with salad dressing.
3. Mesh the salad gently before serving.

Per serving: 175 calories, 2.5g protein, 16.3g carbs, 14.5g fat, 5.6g fiber, 0mg cholesterol, 31mg sodium, 535mg potassium.

Tomato Salad

Preparation time: 10 min

Cooking time: 0 min

Servings: 2

Ingredients:

- 1 red onion, sliced
- 2 cups cherry tomatoes, halved
- ¼ teaspoon ground black pepper
- ½ cup fresh cilantro, chopped
- 1 tablespoon olive oil
- ½ teaspoon dried oregano
- 1 tablespoon apple cider vinegar

Directions:

1. Mix up sliced red onion and cherry tomatoes.
2. Add cilantro. Mix up the salad.
3. Then, sprinkle the salad with apple cider vinegar, ground black pepper, olive oil and dried oregano.

4. Shake the salad gently.

Per serving: 110 calories, 2.4g protein, 12.8g carbs, 7.5g fat, 3.7g fiber, 0mg cholesterol, 13mg sodium, 543mg potassium.

Cheese & Steak Salad

Preparation time: 10 min

Cooking time: 18 min

Servings: 7

Ingredients:

- 10 oz beef sirloin steak
- 1 teaspoon beef seasonings
- 3 cups Romaine lettuce, chopped
- 1 cup sweet pepper, chopped
- 7 oz low-fat cheese, crumbled
- 1 cup cucumbers, chopped
- 1 tablespoon olive oil
- 1 teaspoon avocado oil
- 1 teaspoon balsamic vinegar

Directions:

1. Rub the beef sirloin steak with avocado oil and beef seasonings.
2. Preheat the grill to 400°F and put the steak in it.
3. Cook it for 10 minutes from each side.
4. When the steak is cooked, slice it and place it in the salad bowl.
5. Add cucumbers, romaine lettuce, sweet pepper and shake well.
6. Spray the salad with olive oil and balsamic vinegar.
7. Top the salad with cheese.

Per serving: 199 calories, 19.7g protein, 3g carbs, 14.1g fat, 0.5g fiber, 66mg cholesterol, 205mg sodium, 281mg potassium.

Corn Salad with Spinach

Preparation time: 5 min

Cooking time: 0 min

Servings: 3

Ingredients:

- 1 cup corn kernels, cooked
- 1 teaspoon low-fat sour cream
- 1 cup fresh spinach, chopped
- ½ cup celery stalk, chopped

Directions:

1. Mix up celery stalk, corn kernels and spinach in the salad bowl.
2. Drizzle the cooked salad with low-fat sour cream.

Per serving: 50 calories, 2.1g protein, 10.6g carbs, 1g fat, 1.9g fiber, 1mg cholesterol, 30mg sodium, 240mg potassium.

Shredded Beef Salad

Preparation time: 10 min

Cooking time: 0 min

Servings: 4

Ingredients

- 8 oz beef sirloin, cooked, shredded

- 1 tablespoon mustard
- 1 bell pepper, sliced
- 2 cups lettuce, chopped
- 1 teaspoon lime juice

Directions:

1. In a large bowl, mix up bell pepper, lettuce, and shredded beef sirloin.
2. Sprinkle the salad with mustard and lime juice.

Per serving: 121 calories, 17.3g protein, 4.3g carbs, 4.5g fat, 1g fiber, 51mg cholesterol, 40mg sodium, 345mg potassium.

Tangerine and Edamame Salad

Preparation time: 10 min

Cooking time: 10 min

Servings: 4

Ingredients:

- ½ cup edamame beans, soaked
- 2 cups of water
- 1 cup corn kernels, cooked
- ½ cup Italian parsley, chopped
- 1 tablespoon olive oil
- 1 teaspoon chili flakes
- ½ teaspoon ground black pepper
- 1 cup tangerines, peeled

Directions:

1. Pour water into the skillet. Pour edamame beans and boil them for 10 minutes.
2. Then, drain and rinse the edamame beans and transfer them to the salad bowl.
3. Add cooked corn kernels, parsley, and tangerines.
4. Then spray the salad with ground black pepper, chili flakes, and olive oil.
5. Mix the salad.

Per serving: 110 calories, 7g protein, 15.8g carbs, 5g fat, 2.8g fiber, 0mg cholesterol, 17mg sodium, 234mg potassium.

Chicken Salad in Jars

Preparation time: 10 min

Cooking time: 0 min

Servings: 4

Ingredients:

- 1 cup apples, chopped
- ½ cup grapes halved
- 1 cup lettuce, chopped
- 1-pound chicken breast, boiled, chopped
- ¼ cup low-fat Greek yogurt
- ½ teaspoon ground black pepper
- ¼ teaspoon ground paprika
- 1 teaspoon lemon juice

Directions:

1. Make the dressing: mix lemon juice, ground paprika, ground black pepper, and Greek yogurt.
2. Then pour the dressing into jars.
3. Add the layer of apples, grapes, then lettuce and chicken.
4. Top the salad jars with the yogurt dressing.

Per serving: 154 calories, 25g protein, 13.2g carbs, 3.2g fat, 1.7g fiber, 73mg cholesterol, 68mg sodium, 556mg potassium.

Farro Salad

Preparation time: 10 min

Cooking time: 30 min

Servings: 3

Ingredients:

- 1 cup arugula, chopped
- 3 oz walnuts, chopped
- 1 apple, chopped
- 1 cup of water
- ½ cup farro
- 1 teaspoon honey
- 1 tablespoon low-fat sour cream
- ¼ teaspoon chili powder

Directions:

1. Mix up water and farro.
2. Cook the farro for 30 minutes.
3. Drain the water and place the farro in the bowl.
4. Add walnuts, arugula, apple and mix up the salad.
5. After this, mix up honey, low-fat sour cream, and chili powder in the shallow bowl.
6. Sprinkle the salad with a honey mixture.

Per serving: 309 calories, 12g protein, 37.5g carbs, 17.8g fat, 5.9g fiber, 2mg cholesterol, 30mg sodium, 264mg potassium.

Warm Lentil Salad

Preparation time: 10 min

Cooking time: 15 min

Servings: 6

Ingredients:

- 1 cup green lentils
- 2 cups low-sodium chicken broth
- 1 yellow onion, sliced
- ½ teaspoon dried sage
- 2 tablespoons olive oil
- 1 cup celery stalk, chopped
- 6 oz swiss chard, steamed, chopped
- ½ teaspoon cayenne pepper

Directions:

1. Boil lentils in the chicken broth. Boil it for 15 minutes.
2. After this, transfer the cooked lentils to the salad bowl.
3. Add 1 tablespoon of olive oil.
4. Put the remaining olive oil into the skillet.
5. Then, add sliced yellow onion and cook it until golden brown.
6. Add the cooked onion to the lentils.
7. After this, add celery stalk, swiss chard, cayenne pepper and sage. Stir the salad.

Per serving: 124 calories, 9.8g protein, 23g carbs, 5.2g fat, 11g fiber, 0mg cholesterol, 100mg sodium, 487mg potassium.

Grilled Cod and Blue Cheese Salad

Preparation time: 10 min

Cooking time: 8 min

Servings: 4

Ingredients:

- 1 cup arugula, chopped
- 12 oz cod fillet
- ½ teaspoon ground coriander
- 1 teaspoon apple cider vinegar
- 1 teaspoon olive oil
- 1 tablespoon sesame oil
- ½ teaspoon sesame seeds
- 1 oz blue cheese, crumbled

Directions:

1. Preheat the grill to 390F.
2. Sprinkle the cod fillet with ground coriander, apple cider vinegar and olive oil.
3. Pour the fish fillets in the grill and cook for 4 minutes from each side.
4. Meanwhile, mix up chopped arugula, sesame seeds, blue cheese, and sesame oil in the salad bowl.
5. When the fish is cooked, slice it roughly and add it to the salad. Shake it well.

Per serving: 101 calories, 6.7g protein, 0.5g carbs, 7g fat, 0.1g fiber, 20mg cholesterol, 114mg sodium, 21mg potassium.

Tabbouleh Salad

Preparation time: 10 min

Cooking time: 15 min

Servings: 4

Ingredients:

- ¼ cup bulgur
- 7 oz cucumber, diced
- 3 tomatoes, diced
- ½ cup dill, chopped
- 3 oz scallions, chopped
- ½ teaspoon garlic, diced
- 1 cup of water
- ½ teaspoon chili powder

Directions:

1. Bring to boil the bulgur in water for 15 minutes.
2. Then transfer the cooked bulgur to the bowl.
3. Add diced cucumber, scallions, tomato, dill, garlic, and chili powder.
4. Stir the salad.

Per serving: 71 calories, 3.9g protein, 17.2g carbs, 0.7g fat, 4.5g fiber, 0mg cholesterol, 28mg sodium, 593mg potassium.

Fattoush

Preparation time: 10 min

Cooking time: 0 min

Servings: 2

Ingredients:

- ½ teaspoon sumac
- 1 cup lettuce leaves, chopped
- 1 cup cucumbers, chopped
- 1 cup tomatoes, chopped
- 1 tablespoon fresh mint, chopped
- 2 oz white onion, sliced

- 1 garlic clove, minced
- 2 tablespoons lime juice
- 1 tablespoon apple cider vinegar
- 1 teaspoon olive oil

Directions:

1. For the dressing: mix up apple cider vinegar, minced garlic, lime juice and sumac. Whisk it.
2. Mix up lettuce, fresh mint, cucumbers, tomatoes and white onion in the salad bowl.
3. Mesh the salad ingredients with dressing and mix well.

Per serving: 60 calories, 1.8g protein, 10.7g carbs, 2.7g fat, 2.0g fiber, 0mg cholesterol, 12mg sodium, 406mg potassium.

Couscous Salad

Preparation time: 10 min

Cooking time: 5 min

Servings: 5

Ingredients:

- ½ cup couscous
- 1 cup hot water
- ½ cup chickpeas, canned
- 1 teaspoon olive oil
- ½ teaspoon ground cumin
- 2 cups arugula, chopped
- ¼ cup red onion, chopped
- 3 tablespoon lemon juice
- 3 oz sun-dried tomatoes, sliced

Directions:

1. Pour couscous and chickpeas in the big bowl.
2. Then, add hot water and mix up. Leave it for 5 minutes.
3. Then, add olive oil, ground cumin, arugula, red onion, lemon juice, and sun-dried tomatoes.
4. Stir the salad well.

Per serving: 106 calories, 6.6g protein, 27.3g carbs, 2.5g fat, 4.9g fiber, 0mg cholesterol, 13mg sodium, 298mg potassium.

Bean Salad with Balsamic Vinaigrette

Preparation Time: 15-20 min.

Servings: 6

Ingredients:

The Vinaigrette:

- 2 tablespoon Balsamic vinegar
- 1/3 cup Fresh parsley
- 4 cloves Garlic
- A pinch Ground black pepper
- ¼ cup Olive oil

The Salad:

- 15 oz Black beans – low sodium
- 15 oz Garbanzo beans – low sodium
- 1 Medium red onion
- 6 Lettuce leaves
- ½ cup Celery

Directions:

1. Finely chop the cloves and parsley. Rinse and drain the beans.
2. Finely chop the celery and red onion.

3. Make the vinaigrette by whisking the vinegar with garlic, parsley, and pepper. Whisk in the oil.
4. Toss the onion with the beans and mix in the vinaigrette. Gently toss to combine. Place a lid or foil over the dish and pop it into the fridge for now.
5. Arrange one lettuce leaf on each plate with a portion of the salad - garnishing them using a bit of celery to serve.

Per serving: 206 Calories, 22g Carbs, 10g Fat, 7g Protein, 4g Sugar, 8g Fiber, 174mg Sodium

Warm Rice & Pintos Salad

Preparation Time: 30 min

Servings: 4

Ingredients:

- 1 tablespoon Olive oil
- 1 cup Frozen corn
- 1 Small onion
- 2 Garlic cloves, minced
- 1 ½ teaspoon Ground cumin
- 1 ½ teaspoon Chili powder
- 15 oz Pinto beans
- 8.8 oz Ready-to-serve brown rice
- 4 oz Chopped green chilies
- ½ cup Salsa
- ¼ cup Chopped fresh cilantro
- 1 bunch Romaine - quartered lengthwise through the core
- ¼ cup Finely shredded cheddar cheese

Directions:

1. Prep a big skillet to warm the oil using the med-high temperature setting.
2. Rinse and drain the beans. Chop and mix in the corn and onion. Simmer and stir until the onion are tender (4-5 min.).
3. Mix in the garlic, cumin, and chili powder, stirring for one minute longer.
4. Add beans, rice, green chilies, salsa, and cilantro; heat through, stirring occasionally.
5. Serve over romaine wedges. Sprinkle it with cheese.

Per serving: 331 Calories, 50g Carbs, 8g Fat, 12g Protein, 5g Sugar, 9g Fiber, 465mg Sodium

Celeriac Salad

Preparation time: 5 min

Cooking time: 0 min

Servings: 4

Ingredients:

- 1 cup carrot, shredded
- 1 cup celery root, grated
- 1 oz raisins
- ½ cup apples, grated
- 1 teaspoon olive oil
- 1 teaspoon liquid honey

Directions:

1. Stir carrot, celery root, raisins, and apples.
2. Mix up olive oil and liquid honey.
3. Spray the salad with the oily mixture.

Per serving: 59 calories, 1.1g protein, 17.2g carbs, 1.4g fat, 2.3g fiber, 0mg cholesterol, 59mg sodium, 289mg potassium.

Crunchy Lettuce Salad

Preparation time: 5 min

Cooking time: 0 min

Servings: 3

Ingredients:

- 2 cups lettuce, chopped
- 1 cup cucumbers, chopped
- ½ cup fresh dill, chopped
- 1 orange, peeled, sliced
- 1 tablespoon olive oil
- 1 teaspoon apple cider vinegar

Directions:

1. Mix up dill, lettuce, cucumbers and sprinkle with olive oil and apple cider vinegar in the salad bowl.
2. Garnish the salad with sliced orange.

Per serving: 70 calories, 2.6g protein, 14.1g carbs, 5.2g fat, 3g fiber, 0mg cholesterol, 19mg sodium, 480mg potassium.

Herbed Melon Salad

Preparation time: 5 min

Cooking time: 0 min

Servings: 5

Ingredients:

- 2 cups melon, chopped
- ¼ cup grapes, chopped
- 1 cup cucumbers, chopped
- 3 oz low-fat feta cheese, chopped
- 1 teaspoon Italian seasonings
- ¼ teaspoon ground black pepper
- ¼ cup of orange juice
- 1 tablespoon avocado oil

Directions:

1. Stir melon, grapes, cucumbers, Italian seasonings, and ground black pepper.
2. Then add orange juice and avocado oil. Stir the salad well.
3. Drizzle the cooked salad with chopped low-fat feta cheese.

Per serving: 75 calories, 3.2g protein, 9g carbs, 4.5g fat, 0.9g fiber, 16mg cholesterol, 201mg sodium, 252mg potassium.

Spring Greens Salad

Preparation time: 5 min

Cooking time: 0 min

Servings: 2

Ingredients:

- ½ cup radish, sliced
- 1 cup fresh spinach, chopped
- ½ cup green peas, cooked
- ½ lemon
- 1 cup arugula, chopped
- 1 tablespoon avocado oil
- ½ teaspoon dried sage

Directions:

1. Stir radish, spinach, green peas, arugula, and dried sage in the salad bowl.
2. Then squeeze the lemon over the salad.
3. Then, add avocado oil and shake the salad.

Per serving: 34 calories, 3.1g protein, 9g carbs, 1.3g fat, 3.6g fiber, 0mg cholesterol, 28mg sodium, 321mg potassium.

Apple Salad with Figs & Almonds

Preparation Time: 5-6 min.

Servings: 6

Ingredients:

- 4 cups Red apples, cored and diced
- 1 cup Dried figs
- ¾ cup Carrots
- 2 cups Celery
- ½ cup Fat-free lemon yogurt
- 2 tablespoon Slivered almonds

Directions:

1. Remove the core and dice the apples.
2. Chop the figs and dice the celery.
3. Peel and grate the carrots.
4. Toss the celery with the figs, apples, and carrots.
5. Mix in the yogurt, top with slivered almonds and serve.

Per serving: 93 Calories, 19g Carbs, 1g Fat, 2g Protein, 3g Fiber, 33mg Sodium

Asian Vegetable Salad

Preparation Time: 10 min

Servings: 4

Ingredients:

- 1 ½ cups Carrot
- 1 cup Red cabbage
- ½ cup Julienned red bell pepper
- 1 ½ cups Spinach
- 1 ½ cups Bok choy
- 1 tablespoon Cilantro
- ½ cup Yellow onion
- 1 tablespoon Garlic
- 1 ½ tablespoon Cashews
- 1 ½ cups Snow peas
- 2 teaspoon Soy sauce – low sodium
- 2 teaspoon Toasted sesame oil

Directions:

1. Rinse the veggies using cold running water. Place them in a colander to drain.
2. Julienne (like matchsticks) the pepper, carrot, onion, and bok choy. Chiffonade (cut across the grain - narrow strips) the spinach, cabbage, and cilantro. Mince the garlic.
3. Toss the cut veggies with the garlic, chopped cashews, and snow peas in a large mixing container.
4. Spritz using the oil and a portion of soy sauce over the salad.
5. Toss thoroughly and serve.

Per serving: 113 Calories, 14g Carbs, 4g Fat, 3g Protein, 6g Sugar, 4g Fiber, 168mg Sodium

Tuna Salad

Preparation time: 7 min

Cooking time: 0 min

Servings: 4

Ingredients:

- ½ cup low-fat Greek yogurt
- 8 oz tuna, canned
- ½ cup fresh parsley, chopped
- 1 cup corn kernels, cooked
- ½ teaspoon ground black pepper

Directions:

1. Stir tuna, parsley, kernels, and ground black pepper.
2. Then, add yogurt and mix the salad until it is homogenous.

Per serving: 152 calories,17.8g protein, 13.6g carbs, 5.5g fat, 1.4g fiber, 19mg cholesterol, 55mg sodium, 392mg potassium.

Fish Salad

Preparation time: 5 min

Cooking time: 0 min

Servings: 4

Ingredients:

- 7 oz canned salmon, shredded
- 1 tablespoon lime juice
- 1 tablespoon low-fat yogurt
- 1 cup baby spinach, chopped
- 1 teaspoon capers, drained and chopped

Directions:

1. Stir all ingredients together and transfer them to the salad bowl.

Per serving: 51 calories,11.1g protein, 0.8g carbs, 3.2g fat, 0.2g fiber, 22mg cholesterol, 52mg sodium, 244mg potassium.

Apple lettuce salad

Preparation time: 20 min

Servings: 4

Ingredients:

- ¼ cup Unsweetened apple juice
- 2 tablespoons Lemon juice
- 1 tablespoon Canola oil
- 2 ¼ teaspoons Brown sugar
- ½ teaspoon Dijon mustard
- ¼ teaspoon Apple pie spice
- 1 medium Red apple, chopped,
- 8 cups Mixed salad greens

Directions:

1. Mix the lemon juice, fruit juice, brown sugar, grease, apple pie, and mustard in a big cup.
2. Attach and powder the apple for flipping. The salad greens are added and blended correctly.

Salmon Salad

Preparation time: 10 min

Cooking time: 0 min

Servings: 3

Ingredients:

- 4 oz canned salmon, flaked
- 1 tablespoon lemon juice
- 2 tablespoons red bell pepper, chopped
- 1 tablespoon red onion, chopped
- 1 teaspoon dill, chopped
- 1 tablespoon olive oil

Directions:

1. Combine all ingredients in the salad bowl.

Per serving: 109 calories, 8.3g protein, 6.6g carbs, 7.3g fat, 1.2g fiber, 17mg cholesterol, 21mg sodium, 317mg potassium.

Arugula Salad with Shallot

Preparation time: 10 min

Cooking time: 0 min

Servings: 4

Ingredients:

- 1 cup cucumber, chopped
- 1 tablespoon lemon juice
- 1 tablespoon avocado oil
- 2 shallots, chopped
- ½ cup black olives, sliced
- 3 cups arugula, chopped

Directions:

1. Combine all the ingredients from the previous list in the salad bowl and refrigerate for 5 minutes.

Per serving: 30 calories, 0.8g protein, 2.9g carbs, 2.4g fat, 1.1g fiber, 0mg cholesterol, 152mg sodium, 112mg potassium.

Berry Salad with Shrimps

Preparation time: 7 min

Cooking time: 0 min

Servings: 4

Ingredients:

- 1 cup corn kernels, cooked
- 1 endive, shredded
- 1-pound shrimp, cooked
- 1 tablespoon lime juice
- 2 cups raspberries, halved
- 2 tablespoons olive oil
- 1 tablespoon parsley, chopped

Directions:

1. Pour all ingredients from the list above in the bowl and shake well.

Per serving: 253 calories, 29.5g protein, 21.2g carbs, 10.1g fat, 9.1g fiber, 239mg cholesterol, 313mg sodium, 803mg potassium.

Poultry

BBQ Basil Turkey Burgers

Preparation Time: 30 min.

Servings: 4

Ingredients:

- ¼ cup Fresh basil
- 3 tablespoon BBQ sauce - mesquite smoke-flavor
- 2 tablespoon Oat bran/quick-cooking oats
- 1 Garlic clove
- 1/8 teaspoon Black pepper
- ¼ teaspoon Garlic salt
- 1 lb Lean ground turkey
- 4 Multigrain/Whole-wheat burger buns - split

Optional Garnishes:

- Red onion slices
- Sliced tomato
- Sliced provolone cheese
- Additional barbecue sauce
- Fresh basil leaves

Directions:

1. Mince the garlic. Combine freshly chopped basil with the barbecue sauce, garlic, oats, pepper, and garlic salt. Mix in the turkey, shaping it into four patties (½-inch-thick). Lightly grease a grill rack.
2. Grill the burgers with the top on using the medium-temperature setting until a thermometer reads 165° Fahrenheit/74° Celsius (5-7 min. per side).
3. Slice the buns and grill them using the medium-temperature setting with the cut side down until toasted (30 sec. to 1 min.)
4. Serve the burgers on toasted buns with the toppings of your choice.

Per serving: 315 Calories, 29g Carbs, 11g Fat, 27g Protein, 8g Sugar, 4g Fiber, 482mg Sodium

---

Basic Roast Chicken Breast

Preparation time: 30 min

Servings: 6

Ingredients:

- Olive oil in a pump sprayer
- 2 tablespoons dry vermouth
- ½ teaspoon kosher salt
- ¼ teaspoon freshly ground black pepper
- 1 tablespoon cold unsalted butter (optional)
- 1 tablespoon minced shallot
- 2 (10-oz) chicken breast halves, with bone and skin
- 1 ⅔ cup Homemade Chicken Broth or canned low-sodium chicken broth

Directions:

1. Preheat the oven to 400 F.
2. Use a knife to cut into the skin of the meat and pull back the skin, leaving it attached to the large side of the chicken half. Deal on one breast half at a time: beginning at the rib cage. Season the salt and pepper with the raw skin. Replace the flesh-covering skin.
1. 3. Arrange the side of the chicken skin in a small roasting pan (a 9 or 13-inch metal baking dish works well) and spray the oil. Roast for 35 to 40 minutes before an instant-read thermometer inserted into the thickest part of the chicken registers 165 ° F. Switch the chicken to a carving board for 5 minutes and let it stand. (Let it cool completely if you prepare the chicken

specifically for salads and sandwiches. You can want to skip the next step.)

3. Pour all but 1 teaspoon of the pan's fat off. Add the shallot to the tray and cook over low-medium heat, frequently stirring, for about 1 minute, until the shallot is tender. Connect the broth and bring it to a boil over high heat, scraping the browned bits in the pan with a wooden spoon. Boil until one-third, around 2 minutes, of the broth is reduced. Remove yourself from the sun. Apply the butter to the pan sauce and whisk until the butter melts if you want to thicken the sauce slightly.
4. Carve the chicken meat, discarding the skin and bones. Move and drizzle to dinner plates.
5. Over each serving, equal quantities of sauce. Serve hot.

Chicken Skillet

Preparation time: 10 min

Cooking time: 26 min

Servings: 6

Ingredients:

- 4 chicken fillets
- 1 teaspoon ground black pepper
- ½ teaspoon ground paprika
- 1 tablespoon olive oil
- 3 oz low-fat sour cream
- 1 cup asparagus, chopped
- ¼ cup of water

Directions:

1. Slice the chicken fillet and drizzle it with paprika and ground black pepper.
2. Pour the sliced chicken in the skillet, add olive oil, and cook it for 3 minutes from each side.
3. Then add low-fat sour cream and asparagus.
4. Add water and close the lid.
5. Sauté the meal for 20 minutes.

Per serving: 231 calories, 29.2g protein, 1.8g carbs, 12.6g fat, 0.6g fiber, 93mg cholesterol, 92mg sodium, 311mg potassium.

Turkey Stir-Fry

Preparation time: 10 min

Cooking time: 25 min

Servings: 5

Ingredients:

- 12 oz turkey fillet, sliced
- 1 carrot, julienned
- 1 onion, sliced
- 1 teaspoon potato starch
- ½ cup low-sodium chicken broth
- 1 tablespoon avocado oil
- 1 teaspoon chili powder

Directions:

1. Pour avocado oil in the skillet and add turkey fillet.
2. Roast the poultry for 4 minutes (2 minutes from each side).
3. Then add chili powder, carrot and onion. Mix the ingredients and cook them for 10 minutes.
4. Then, mix up potato starch and chicken broth.
5. Put the liquid over the turkey mixture and stir well.

6. Cook the meal for 10 mins more.

Per serving: 81 calories, 14.8g protein, 4.8g carbs, 0.8g fat, 1.1g fiber, 35mg cholesterol, 176mg sodium, 90mg potassium.

Chicken and Low-fat Goat Cheese Bowl

Preparation time: 10 min

Cooking time: 20 min

Servings: 4

Ingredients:

- 1-pound chicken breast, skinless, boneless, chopped
- 2 tomatoes, chopped
- 3 oz low-fat goat cheese, crumbled
- ½ teaspoon ground black pepper
- ¼ teaspoon garlic powder
- 1 tablespoon olive oil
- 1 tablespoon lemon juice

Directions:

1. Stir the chicken with olive oil, lemon juice, garlic powder, and ground black pepper.
2. Then transfer the chicken to the baking tray, flatten it well and bake at 400F for 20 minutes.
3. Then, put the chicken in the serving bowls and top with low-fat goat cheese and tomatoes.

Per serving: 259 calories, 31.2g protein, 3.2g carbs, 14.1g fat, 0.9g fiber, 95mg cholesterol, 135mg sodium, 586mg potassium.

Chicken Chop Suey

Preparation time: 10 min

Cooking time: 35 min

Servings: 4

Ingredients:

- ¼ cup reduced-sodium soy sauce
- 1-pound chicken fillet, chopped
- ½ cup mushrooms, chopped
- ½ onion, chopped
- ½ teaspoon chili flakes
- 2 tablespoons avocado oil
- 1 cup bean sprouts, canned

Directions:

1. Heat avocado oil in the deep skillet.
2. Then, add mushrooms and roast them for 3 minutes.
3. After this, add chopped onion, stir the vegetables and cook them for 7 minutes. Mix them from time to time to avoid burning.
4. Transfer the cooked vegetables to the serving bowls.
5. Then add chicken to the skillet and sprinkle it with chili flakes. Cook it for 15 minutes. Stir it occasionally.
6. Then add the bean sprouts and cook the meal for another 10 minutes.
7. Transfer the mixture over the mushroom-onion mixture.

Per serving: 179 calories, 24.1g protein, 3.5g carbs, 6.4g fat, 0.6g fiber, 67mg cholesterol, 422mg sodium, 307mg potassium.

Classic Poached Chicken

Preparation time: 30 min

Servings: 2

Ingredients:

- ½ Cups diced chicken meat
- 2 (10-ounce) chicken breast halves, with bone and skin
- 1 small onion, thinly sliced
- 2 sprigs of fresh parsley (optional)
- Pinch of dried thyme
- A few black peppercorns
- ½ bay leaf

Directions:

1. Place the chicken and onion in a medium saucepan and add ample water to cover 1 inch (about 1quart). Bring over high heat to a simmer, skimming off any foam growing to the surface.
2. Attach the parsley, thyme, peppercorns, and bay leaf (if used). Simmer for 15 minutes and reduce the heat to medium-low. The chicken won't be cooked thoroughly.
3. Remove from the heat and tightly cover. When pierced at the thickest part with the tip of a knife, let stand till the chicken is opaque, about 20 minutes. Put chicken on a cutting board and let cool until easy to handle.
4. Pull the bones and skin off. (Return the skin and bones to the skillet dish if you want to make chicken stock. Boil over low heat until the liquid is reduced to around 2 cups, about 1 hour. Drain into a heatproof bowl and cool. Refrigerate for up to 3-days in an airtight jar or freeze for up to 2 months.)

Seal and refrigerate the meat for up to 2 days.

Chicken Mediterranean with Artichokes and Rosemary

Preparation time: 30 Minutes

Servings: 2

Ingredients:

- 1 tablespoon olive oil, plus more in a pump sprayer
- 2 (12-ounce) boneless, skinless chicken breasts, pounded to even thickness, each cut in half crosswise to make 4 serving piece
- 1 teaspoon kosher salt
- ¼ teaspoon freshly ground black pepper
- ½ small yellow onion, chopped
- ½ large red bell pepper, cut into ½-inch dice, seeded
- 1 clove garlic, minced1 (14.5-ounce) no-salt-added diced tomatoes in juice, drained1 (9-ounce) box thawed frozen artichoke hearts, coarsely chopped
- 2 teaspoons cornstarch
- 1 cup Homemade Chicken Broth or canned low-sodium chicken broth
- 2 teaspoons chopped fresh rosemary or sage, or 1 teaspoon dried rosemary or sage
- ¼ teaspoon crushed hot red pepper

Directions:

1. Sprinkle a large nonstick skillet over medium heat with oil and heat. With salt and pepper, season the chicken. Then, add the chicken to the casserole and cook for about 7 minutes, turning halfway through

the cooking procedure until golden brown on both sides. Transfer to a dish.
2. Heat 1 tablespoon oil over medium heat in a skillet. Add the garlic, onion, bell pepper, and cook for about 5 minutes, occasionally stirring, until tender. Stir in the artichokes and tomatoes. Dissolve the cornstarch into the broth in a small bowl. Stir, along with the rosemary and hot pepper, into the skillet mixture. Pour the chicken back in the skillet and bring the liquid down to a simmer. Lower the heat to medium-low and cover the skillet with the garlic lid. Cook until juices are slightly thickened, and the chicken is opaque when pierced with the tip of a knife in the thickest portion, around 6 minutes, stirring occasionally. Serve it warm.

Chicken Packets

Preparation time: 15 min

Cooking time: 35 min

Servings: 3

Ingredients:

- 12 oz chicken fillet
- 2 sweet peppers, sliced
- 1 red onion, sliced
- 1 teaspoon Italian seasonings
- 2 tablespoons olive oil
- 1 tomato, sliced
- 3 tablespoons apple cider vinegar

Directions:

1. Cut the chicken fillet on 3 servings.
2. Then put them into the 3 baking packets.
3. Add sliced sweet pepper, Italian seasonings, onion, olive oil, tomato, and apple cider vinegar. Secure the packets and shake well.
4. Preheat the oven to 385F.
5. Pour the chicken packets in the tray and bake them for 40 minutes.

Per serving: 340 calories, 34.2g protein, 10.2g carbs, 18.5g fat, 2.1g fiber, 102mg cholesterol, 103mg sodium, 539mg potassium.

Herbed Chicken Breast

Preparation time: 10 min

Cooking time: 45 min

Servings: 4

Ingredients:

- 1-pound chicken breast
- 1 teaspoon dried sage
- 1 teaspoon dried basil
- 1 teaspoon ground paprika
- 1 teaspoon dried oregano
- ¼ teaspoon cumin seeds
- 2 tablespoons margarine, melted

Directions:

1. In the shallow bowl, paprika, mix up sage, basil, oregano and cumin seeds.
2. Rub the chicken with the spice mixt and then brush well with the melted margarine.
3. Wrap the chicken breast in foil and bake in the preheated 375°F oven for 45 minutes.

Per serving: 181 calories, 22.3g protein, 0.8g carbs, 8.7g fat, 0.4g fiber, 73mg cholesterol, 125mg sodium, 446mg potassium.

Chinese Chicken with Bok Choy and Garlic

Preparation time: 30 Minutes

Servings: 4

Ingredients:

Sauce:

- ¾ cup Homemade Chicken Broth or canned low-sodium chicken broth
- 2 tablespoons rice vinegar
- 1 tablespoon reduced-sodium soy sauce
- 1 teaspoon amber agave nectar or sugar
- ½ teaspoon crushed hot red pepper
- 2 teaspoons cornstarch

Chicken:

- 4 teaspoons canola oil
- 1-pound boneless, skinless chicken breast halves, cut across the grain into ¼-inch-thick slices
- 4 cloves garlic, minced
- 2 tablespoons peeled and minced fresh ginger
- 1 large head bok choy (1½ pounds), cut crosswise into ½-inch-thick pieces, well washed, but not dried
- 3 scallions, green and white parts, slice into 1-inch lengths

Directions:

1. To make the sauce: Combine the broth, vinegar, soy sauce, agave, and hot pepper in a small cup. Sprinkle and whisk in the cornstarch to dissolve. Put aside the mixture for the sauce.
2. Heat 2 teaspoons of oil over medium-high heat in a large wok or nonstick skillet to cook the chicken. Add the chicken and cook for about 2 minutes, occasionally stirring, until lightly browned. Transfer to a dish.
3. Heat the skillet with the remaining 2 teaspoons of oil. Apply the garlic and ginger and mix for about 30 seconds until it is fragrant. Add the scallions, bok choy and cook for about 3 minutes, frequently stirring, until the bok choy is crisp-tender. Return the chicken and any juices back in the pan on the counter. Cook, constantly stirring, until the whole chicken is opaque, around 1 minute. Stir in the mixture of the sauce and cook, continually stirring, until cooked and slightly thickened. Serve it warm.

Chicken with Mushroom Cacciatore Sauce

Preparation time: 30 Min

Servings: 4

Ingredients:

- 1 tablespoon olive oil, plus more in a pump sprayer
- 2 (12-ounce) boneless, skinless chicken breast halves, pounded to even thickness, each cut in half crosswise to make 4 serving pieces
- ½ teaspoon kosher salt
- ¼ teaspoon freshly ground black pepper
- 1 medium yellow onion, chopped
- ½ medium bell pepper (green), cored and cut into ½-inch dice
- 1 clove garlic, minced

- 1 (14.5-ounce) can no-salt-added diced tomatoes with juice, undrained ¼ cup hearty red wine, dry vermouth, or water
- 1 teaspoon Italian herb seasoning or dried oregano

Directions:

1. Sprinkle a large nonstick skillet over medium heat with oil and heat. Season the chicken with pepper and salt, add to the skillet, and cook until golden brown on both sides, around 6 minutes, turning halfway through cooking. Transfer to a dish.
2. Warm 2 tablespoon oil over medium heat in a skillet. Add the garlic, bell pepper, onion and cook for about 5 minutes, occasionally stirring, until tender. Then, add the wine, the tomatoes and their juice and the seasoning of the herbs. Bring to a boil, scrape with a wooden spoon the browned bits in the skillet. Decrease the heat to med-low and simmer for about 5 mins until the liquid is slightly reduced.
3. Return the chicken back in the casserole and cover it with a garlic lid. When pierced in the thickest part with the tip of a sharp knife, boil until the chicken becomes opaque, 6 to 8 minutes. Serve it wet.

Chicken and Vegetables Wraps

Preparation time: 10 min

Cooking time: 8 min

Servings: 3

Ingredients:

- 3 lettuce leaves
- 9 oz chicken fillet
- 1 teaspoon rotisserie chicken seasonings
- 3 celery stalks
- 1 carrot, cut into sticks
- 3 teaspoons low-fat yogurt
- 1 tablespoon olive oil

Directions:

1. Cut the chicken and pour it in the skillet.
2. Add olive oil and cook it for 4 mins from each side, until the chicken slices are light brown.
3. Let cool the chicken gently and place it on the lettuce leaves.
4. Add carrot and celery stalks. Drizzle the ingredients with yogurt and wrap.

Per serving: 210 calories, 25.2g protein, 3g carbs, 11.1g fat, 0.8g fiber, 76mg cholesterol, 122mg sodium, 335mg potassium.

Sesame Shredded Chicken

Preparation time: 10 min

Cooking time: 20 min

Servings: 2

Ingredients:

- 10 oz chicken breast, skinless, boneless
- 1 cup of water
- 1 teaspoon sesame seeds
- 1 teaspoon sesame oil
- 1 tomato, chopped
- ½ teaspoon cayenne pepper

Directions:

1. Pour the chicken breast in water and boil it for 15 minutes.

2. Then drain water and shred the chicken.
3. Transfer the shredded chicken to the skillet.
4. Add sesame oil, cayenne pepper, and tomato.
5. Cook the shredded chicken for 5 minutes.
6. top the cooked meal with sesame seeds.

Per serving: 188 calories, 30.6g protein, 1.8g carbs, 6.7g fat, 0.7g fiber, 91mg cholesterol, 78mg sodium, 615mg potassium.

Chicken Piccata

Preparation time: 10 min

Cooking time: 12 min

Servings: 3

Ingredients:

- 9 oz chicken fillet
- 1 tablespoon whole-grain wheat flour
- 1 teaspoon ground black pepper
- 3 tablespoons lemon juice
- 1/3 cup low-sodium chicken stock
- 1 teaspoon margarine
- 1 tablespoon capers

Directions:

1. Cut the chicken fillet and sprinkle with flour.
2. Melt the margarine in the casserole, add chicken and roast it for 2 minutes from each side.
3. After this, add lemon juice, ground black pepper, chicken stock, and capers.
4. Mix the chicken well and close the lid.
5. Cook the chicken piccata for 8 minutes more.

Per serving: 200 calories, 25.3g protein, 2.7g carbs, 7.8g fat, 0.7g fiber, 76mg cholesterol, 192mg sodium, 246mg potassium.

Lean Chicken Thighs

Preparation time: 10 min

Cooking time: 25 min

Servings: 4

Ingredients:

- ½ teaspoon ground black pepper
- ½ teaspoon ground paprika
- ½ teaspoon garlic powder
- 1 tablespoon sesame oil
- 4 chicken thighs, boneless, skinless

Directions:

1. Rub the chicken thighs with paprika, ground black pepper and garlic powder.
2. Heat the skillet and pour oil inside.
3. Then, add chicken thighs and cook them for 10 minutes. Turn the chicken over and cook for another 10 minutes.

Per serving: 280 calories, 42.4g protein, 0.6g carbs, 14.3g fat, 0.2g fiber, 130mg cholesterol, 126mg sodium, 368mg potassium.

Blackened Chicken

Preparation time: 10 min

Cooking time: 25 min

Servings: 2

Ingredients:

- 8 oz chicken fillet
- ½ teaspoon ground coriander
- ½ teaspoon ground cumin
- 1 teaspoon ground paprika
- 1 teaspoon dried oregano
- ½ teaspoon ground black pepper
- 1 tablespoon olive oil
- 1 teaspoon water

Directions:

1. Cut the chicken fillet into 2 servings and sprinkle with water.
2. In the salad bowl, mix up all spices from the list above.
3. Heat the olive oil in the skillet.
4. Then Sprinkle the chicken fillets with the spice mix and put in the hot oil.
5. Roast chicken for 10 minutes (5 from each side) and then transfer it to the baking pan and cook for 15 minutes more at 385°F.

Per serving: 280calories, 33.2g protein, 1.6g carbs, 15.8g fat, 0.9g fiber, 101mg cholesterol, 99mg sodium, 329mg potassium.

Chicken and Apple Curry

Preparation time: 30 min

Servings: 4

Ingredients:

- 2 teaspoons canola oil, plus more in a pump sprayer
- 2 (10-ounce) boneless, skinless chicken breast halves, trimmed, pounded to ¾-inch thickness, and cut into 4 equal serving portions
- 1 medium yellow onion, chopped
- 2 medium celery ribs, chopped
- 2 apples (Granny Smith), cored, peeled and diced into ½-inch
- 1 tablespoon curry powder
- ¾ cup light coconut milk
- ½ cup of water
- 2 tablespoons fresh lime juice
- ½ cup sliced natural almonds, for serving

Directions:

1. Spray the wide nonstick skillet over medium-high heat with oil and heat. Add the chicken and cook for about 6 minutes, flipping halfway through cooking until lightly browned on both sides. Transfer to a dish.
2. Heat 2 teaspoons of oil over low-medium heat in a skillet. Add the onion, celery, and apples and cook for about 5 minutes, frequently stirring, until the onion is tender. Sprinkle and mix well with the curry powder.
3. Stir in the coconut milk, lime juice, and water and bring to a boil, stirring frequently. Stir in the chicken and cover. When pierced in the center with the sharp of a knife, reduce the heat to medium-low and simmer until the chicken is opaque around 6 minutes.
4. Move the chicken to a deep serving platter. Increase the heat to high and boil the sauce for around 1 minute until slightly thickened. Over the chicken, pour in the sauce mixture and sprinkle with the almonds. Serve hot.

"Moo Shu" Chicken and Vegetable Wraps

Preparation time: 30 min

Servings: 6

Ingredients:

Sauce:

- ⅓ cup Homemade Chicken Broth or canned low-sodium chicken broth
- 1 tablespoon rice vinegar
- 1 tablespoon no-salt-added tomato ketchup
- 1 tablespoon reduced-sodium soy sauce
- 1 teaspoon Asian sesame oil
- 2 teaspoons cornstarch

Chicken:

- 4 teaspoons canola oil
- 1 (8-oz) boneless, skinless chicken breast half, cut across the grain into ¼-inch-thick bite-sized pieces
- 10 ounces shiitake mushroom caps, sliced
- 1 (12-ounce) package broccoli slaw
- 3 scallions, green and white parts, slice into 1-inch lengths
- 1 (8-ounce) can sliced water chestnuts, drained and rinsed
- 1 tablespoon peeled and minced fresh ginger
- 2 cloves garlic, minced

Wraps:

- 12 Boston or Bibb lettuce leaves

Directions:

1. To make the sauce: whisk the broth, vinegar, ketchup, soy sauce, sesame oil, and cornstarch together in a small bowl.
2. To cook the chicken: Heat 2 teaspoons of oil over medium to high heat in a large nonstick skillet. Add the chicken and cook, stirring periodically, for about 4 minutes, until it becomes opaque. Transfer to a dish. In the casserole, heat the remaining 2 teaspoons of oil over medium to high heat. Add the mushrooms and cook for about 5 minutes, occasionally stirring, until tender. Add the broccoli slaw, scallions, and water chestnuts and cook for about 3 minutes, frequently stirring, until the slaw is hot and wilted. Then, add the garlic, fresh ginger and cook for another 1 minute, until fragrant. Stir in the reserved sauce and chicken.
3. Blend and apply to the skillet. Mix for about 30 seconds until the sauce is thickened and heated.
4. Move the chicken mixture to a mixing bowl to eat. Let each person spoon the chicken mixture onto a lettuce leaf, roll it up and enjoy it.

Roast Turkey Breast with Root Vegetables, Lemon, and Garlic Cloves

Preparation time: 30 min

Servings: 6

Ingredients:

- 1 (2¾-pound) turkey breast half, with skin and bones
- 1 teaspoon Italian Seasoning or herbes de Provence
- 1 teaspoon kosher salt

- ¾ teaspoon freshly ground black pepper
- 2 pounds red-skinned potatoes, Diced into 1-inch pieces
- 3 large carrots, cut into 1-inch pieces
- 1 turnip, peeled and diced into 1-inch pieces
- 2 medium parsnips, peeled and cut into 1-inch pieces
- 1 head garlic, separated into unpeeled cloves
- 1 tablespoon olive oil
- Grated zest of 1 lemon
- 2 tablespoons fresh lemon juice
- 1 tablespoon cornstarch
- 1½ cups Homemade Chicken Broth or canned low-sodium chicken broth Chopped fresh parsley for garnish

Directions:

1. Preheat the oven to 350°F.
2. Make a narrow incision in the turkey breast to remove the skin from the rib bones using a thin, sharp knife. To create a pocket, slip your fingers under the skin. Season the flesh with the herbs of Provence, half a teaspoon of salt, and half a teaspoon of pepper under the surface.
3. Mix the potatoes, carrots, parsnips, turnips, and garlic in a broad roasting pan. Drizzle and toss well with the grease. Spread with the turkey in the pan and roof.
4. In the thickest section of the breast half, roast until the turkey is golden brown and an instant-read thermometer inserted registers 165 °F, around 1½ hours. Pass the turkey on a cutting board and tent with the carving
5. Foil with aluminum.
6. Increase the temperature of the oven to 450°F. In the roasting pan, continue cooking the vegetables, stirring periodically, until tender and lightly browned, for approximately 10 minutes. Take it out of the oven. Add the lemon zest and juice, 1/2 teaspoon salt remaining, and 1/4 teaspoon pepper remaining and toss well. Transfer to an aluminum foil serving platter and tent to stay warm.
7. In the pan, pour out and discard the fat. Sprinkle the cornstarch over the broth in a small bowl and whisk until it is dissolved. Heat the roasting pan until sizzling over medium-high heat. Put in the broth mixture and bring to a boil, scraping with a wooden spoon the browned bits in the pan. Decrease heat to low and cook on low for approximately 2 minutes until slightly thickened. Pour the sauce into a boat with the gravy.
8. Discard the skin of the turkey. In 1/2-inch-thick slices, cut the turkey meat from the bone around the grain. Over the carrots, arrange the turkey and sprinkle with the parsley. With the sauce, serve sweet.

Grilled Chicken Fillets

Preparation time: 15 min

Cooking time: 15 min

Servings: 6

Ingredients:

- 18 oz chicken fillet
- 1 teaspoon cumin seeds
- 2 tablespoons olive oil
- 1/2 teaspoon dried sage
- 1 teaspoon dried basil
- ½ lemon

Directions:

1. Squeeze the lemon-juice into the bowl.
2. Add sage, cumin seeds, olive oil, and basil.
3. Then cut the chicken fillet into 6 servings and place it in the lemon mixture.
4. Marinate the chicken for 10-15 minutes.
5. Meanwhile, preheat the grill to 400F.
6. Place marinated chicken in grill and cook for 7 minutes on each side.
7. Slice the chicken and transfer it to the serving plates.

Per serving: 195 calories, 27.4g protein, 0.6g carbs, 11.1g fat, 0.2g fiber, 76mg cholesterol, 74mg sodium, 221mg potassium.

Oregano Turkey Tenders

Preparation time: 10 min

Cooking time: 10 min

Servings: 4

Ingredients:

- 2 turkey breast fillets, skinless, boneless
- 1 tablespoon dried oregano
- 1 tablespoon olive oil

Directions:

1. Chop the chicken fillets into the tenders and sprinkle with dried oregano and olive oil.
2. Then put the turkey tenders in the casserole in one layer and cook them for 10 minutes (5 minutes from each side) or until the tenders are golden brown.

Per serving: 91 calories, 13.5g protein, 1.2g carbs, 4.8g fat, 0.2g fiber, 30mg cholesterol, 240mg sodium, 6mg potassium.

Turkey Chili

Preparation time: 10 min

Cooking time: 35 min

Servings: 6

Ingredients:

- 2 cups ground turkey
- 1 cup red kidney beans, canned
- 1 cup tomatoes, chopped
- 1 teaspoon chili powder
- ½ teaspoon ground cayenne pepper
- 3 cups of water
- 1 tablespoon margarine
- 1 onion, diced

Directions:

1. Mix margarine in the saucepan and melt it.
2. Then, add onion and cook it for 3 minutes.
3. Then stir it and add ground turkey.
4. Sprinkle the turkey with ground cayenne pepper and chili powder. Mix well and cook for 5 minutes.
5. Add red kidney beans, tomatoes, and water.
6. Cover and cook chili for 30 minutes over medium heat.

Per serving: 319 calories, 37.6g protein, 22g carbs, 14.5g fat, 5.6g fiber, 112mg cholesterol, 154mg sodium, 825mg potassium.

Turkey Bake

Preparation time: 15 min

Cooking time: 45 min

Servings: 4

Ingredients:

- 1 cup broccoli, chopped
- ¼ cup low-fat cheese, shredded
- 1 cup ground turkey
- 1 teaspoon chili flakes
- 1 cup low-fat sour cream
- 1 teaspoon olive oil
- 1 jalapeno pepper, chopped

Directions:

1. Brush the casserole mold with olive oil. Preheat the oven to 390F.
2. Mix up chili flakes, ground turkey and transfer the mixture to the prepared casserole mold. Flatten the mix well.
3. Then, top it with broccoli, jalapeno pepper, and low-fat sour cream.
4. Sprinkle the mixture with the sliced cheese and top with foil.
5. Bake it for 45 minutes.

Per serving: 201 calories, 22.3g protein, 7.8g carbs, 9.2g fat, 0.7g fiber, 64mg cholesterol, 144mg sodium, 335mg potassium.

Turkey Meatloaf

Preparation time: 15 min

Cooking time: 35 min

Servings: 6

Ingredients:

- 1-pound ground turkey
- 2 oz walnuts, chopped
- 1 teaspoon Italian seasonings
- 1 tablespoon potato starch
- 1 tablespoon semolina
- ¼ cup corn kernels
- 1 teaspoon olive oil

Directions:

1. Stir well ground turkey, walnuts, Italian seasonings, potato starch, semolina, and corn kernels in the mixing bowl.
1. Brush the mold with olive oil and pour the turkey mixture inside.
2. Flatten it well and cover it with the foil.
3. Insert the meatloaf in the preheated to 380F oven and cook it 35 minutes.

Per serving: 203 calories, 23.4g protein, 5.2g carbs, 15g fat, 0.9g fiber, 78mg cholesterol, 82mg sodium, 275mg potassium.

Turkey Burgers

Preparation time: 10 min

Cooking time: 10 min

Servings: 3

Ingredients:

- 9 oz ground turkey
- ¼ cup fresh parsley, chopped
- 1 teaspoon minced garlic
- ½ teaspoon chili pepper
- 1 tablespoon semolina
- 1 tablespoon coconut oil

Directions:

1. Mix up ground turkey, garlic, parsley, chili pepper, and semolina.
2. Heat coconut oil in the skillet.
3. Then, make the burgers and put them in the hot coconut oil.
4. Cook the burgers for 8 minutes (4 minutes per side).

Per serving: 201 calories,23.9g protein, 3.3g carbs, 14g fat, 0.4g fiber, 87mg cholesterol, 94mg sodium, 270mg potassium.

Turkey-Spinach Meatballs with Tomato Sauce

Preparation time: 30 Minutes

Servings: 6

Ingredients:

Turkey-Spinach Meatballs:

- 1 (10-oz) box frozen chopped spinach, thawed and squeezed to remove excess liquid
- 1 medium yellow onion, shredded on the large holes of a box grater
- 2 cloves garlic, minced
- ⅓ cup whole-wheat bread crumbs, made from day-old bread pulsed in the blender
- 2 large egg whites or ¼ cup seasoned liquid egg substitute
- 1 teaspoon Italian seasoning or dried oregano
- 1 teaspoon kosher salt
- ½ teaspoon freshly ground black pepper
- 1¼ pounds ground turkey
- Olive oil in a pump sprayer
- ½ cup of water

Tomato Sauce:

- 1 tablespoon olive oil
- 1 medium yellow onion, chopped
- 2 cloves garlic, minced
- 1 (28-ounce) can no-salt-added crushed tomatoes
- 2 teaspoons Italian Seasoning or dried oregano
- ¼ teaspoon ground hot red pepper
- 6 tablespoons freshly grated Parmesan cheese

Directions:

1. Combine the spinach, onion, garlic, bread crumbs, egg whites, Italian seasoning, salt, and pepper in a big bowl to make the meatballs. Attach and thoroughly mix the ground turkey. To firm up the mixture and make it easier to handle, refrigerate it for 15 to 30 minutes.
2. Roll up 18 meatballs with the turkey mixture. Brush a large nonstick skillet over medium heat with oil and heat. In batches, add the meatballs and cook for around 6 minutes, occasionally turning, until lightly browned. Transfer to a dish. Connect the water to the skillet and bring to a boil, using a wooden spoon to stir the browned pieces in the pan.
3. To make the sauce: Heat the oil over medium heat in a medium saucepan. Attach the onion and sauté for about 5 minutes, occasionally stirring, until golden and tender. Mix in the garlic and cook for about a minute until it is fragrant. Add the skillet sauce, onions, Italian seasoning, and hot pepper; thoroughly mix and bring to a boil. Reduce heat to medium-low and

simmer until mildly thickened, occasionally stirring, for about 15 minutes. Bury the meatballs in the sauce and cook until the meatballs, when pierced to the middle with the tip of a sharp knife, show no sign of pink, about 15 more minutes. Divide 6 bowls of meatballs and sauce, sprinkle each with 1 tablespoon of Parmesan cheese (if used), and serve warm.

Cajun Turkey Burgers with Pickled Red Onions

Preparation time: 30 min

Servings: 4

Ingredients:

Pickled Red Onions:

- 1 red onion, cut into thin half-moons
- ½ cup cider vinegar, as needed

Turkey Burgers:

- 2 teaspoons canola oil, plus more in a pump sprayer
- 2 celery ribs, finely chopped
- ½ cup finely chopped red bell pepper
- 2 cloves garlic, finely chopped
- 2 scallions, finely chopped
- 1 teaspoon Cajun Seasoning
- 1¼ pounds ground turkey
- ½ teaspoon kosher salt
- 4 whole-wheat hamburger buns, toasted
- 4 tomato slices
- 4 red lettuce leaves

Directions:

1. To pickle the onions: In a small bowl, put the onions and add enough vinegar to cover the onions. Allow to rest for at least 35 minutes and up to 6 hours at room temperature.
2. To make turkey burgers: Heat 2 teaspoons of oil over medium heat in a large nonstick skillet. Add the celery, garlic and bell pepper and cook for about 5 minutes, occasionally stirring, until tender.
3. Attach the scallions and cook for about 2 minutes until they are wilted. Stir in the Spice of the Cajun. Put it in a large bowl and let it cool. To the vegetable mixture, add the ground turkey and salt and thoroughly blend. Shape into four burgers, 3 1/2-inch. Place it on a plate lined with waxed paper and cook for 15 to 30 minutes.
4. Using paper towels, wash the skillet out. With the grease, spray the skillet and heat over medium heat. Attach the burgers and cook for about 5 minutes until the undersides are golden brown. Flip the burgers and cook until the other sides are browned, and when pushed on top with a finger, the burgers feel resilient, about 5 minutes more. Withdraw from the skillet
5. Place a burger in a bun with each serving and top with some red onions, a tomato, and a lettuce leaf. Serve hot.

Turkey Mini Meat Loaf with Dijon Glaze

Preparation time: 30 min

Servings: 4

Ingredients:

- 2 teaspoons canola oil, plus more in a pump sprayer
- 1 medium yellow onion, finely chopped
- 1 medium carrot, cut into ¼-inch dice
- 1 medium celery stalk, cut into ¼-inch dice
- 1 tablespoon water
- 1¼ pounds ground turkey
- ¾ cup old-fashioned (rolled) oats
- 1 large egg, beaten
- 1 teaspoon dried rosemary
- ½ teaspoon kosher salt
- ¼ teaspoon freshly ground black pepper
- 1 tablespoon Dijon mustard
- 1 tablespoon honey

Directions:

1. Preheat the oven to 350°F. Line with aluminum foil on a large baking sheet and spray with oil.
2. Heat 2 teaspoons of oil over medium heat in a medium nonstick skillet.
3. Add the onion, carrot, water, and celery. Cook, stirring periodically, for about 10 minutes, until the vegetables are tender. Place in a medium bowl and leave to cool slightly. Apply the ground turkey, oats, egg, rosemary, salt, and pepper and blend until mixed, gently but thoroughly. Split into 4 equal portions and form each, about 2 inches apart, into a 5/3-inch loaf on the prepared baking sheet.
4. Bake until lightly browned and placed in the center of a loaf; an instant-read thermometer readsabout160 ° F, about 35 minutes. Take it out of the oven. In a large bowl, put the honey and mustard, then spread the top of each loaf with one-quarter of the mustard mixture. Return to the oven and baking until the mustard mixture is glazed. Leave to stand before serving at room temperature for 5 minutes.

Curry Chicken Wings

Preparation time: 10 min

Cooking time: 25 min

Servings: 4

Ingredients:

- 1-pound chicken wings, skinless, boneless
- 1 teaspoon curry paste
- ½ cup skim milk
- 1 tablespoon coconut oil

Directions:

1. Stir curry paste and skim milk until smooth.
2. Pour the coconut oil in the saucepan and melt it.
3. Then, add the chicken wings and cook them for 4 minutes (2 minutes per side).
4. After this, add mixture and stir the chicken.
5. Close the lid and cook it for 22 minutes on medium-high heat.

Per serving: 250 calories,33.9g protein, 1.9g carbs, 12.5g fat, 0g fiber, 102mg cholesterol, 114mg sodium, 323mg potassium.

Basil Stuffed Chicken Breast

Preparation time: 15 min

Cooking time: 45 min

Servings: 4

Ingredients:

- 1 tomato, sliced
- 1 oz basil leaves
- 1 teaspoon ground black pepper
- 1 tablespoon sesame oil
- 1 teaspoon minced garlic
- 1-pound chicken breast, skinless, boneless

Directions:

1. Cut lengthwise into the chicken breast.
2. Rub the chicken breast with ground black pepper, minced garlic and fill with basil leaves and tomato slices.
3. Secure the cut with toothpicks.
4. Then drizzle the chicken breast with sesame oil and wrap in the foil.
5. Bake the chicken for 45 minutes at 385F.

Per serving: 166 calories, 24.5g protein, 1.4g carbs, 6.3g fat, 0.5g fiber, 73mg cholesterol, 59mg sodium, 487mg potassium.

Tomato Chicken Stew

Preparation time: 10 min

Cooking time: 25 min

Servings: 4

Ingredients:

- 10 oz chicken fillet, chopped
- 2 sweet peppers, chopped
- 1 cup tomatoes, chopped
- 1 chili pepper, chopped
- ¼ cup of water
- 1 teaspoon olive oil

Directions:

1. Heat up olive oil in the skillet.
2. Add sweet pepper and chili pepper. Roast the vegetables for 3 minutes.
3. Then, add chicken and cook the ingredients for 10 mins.
4. Add tomatoes and water.
5. Stir the stew well and cook for another 15 minutes.

Per serving: 165 calories, 21.5g protein, 6.3g carbs, 6.7g fat, 1.4g fiber, 63mg cholesterol, 65mg sodium, 393mg potassium.

Turkey Mix

Preparation time: 5 min

Cooking time: 25 min

Servings: 4

Ingredients:

- 2 tablespoons canola oil
- 1-pound turkey fillet, sliced
- ½ teaspoon ground black pepper
- 3 garlic cloves, minced
- 1 cup artichoke, canned, chopped
- 1 cup low-fat milk

Directions:

1. Heat a pan with the oil over medium-high heat, add sliced turkey, garlic and black pepper, cook the ingredients for 5 minutes.

2. Add the rest of the ingredients, toss gently, and cook over medium heat for 15 minutes.
3. Stir well and cook for another 5 minutes.

Per serving: 220 calories, 30.8g protein, 7.2g carbs, 8.3g fat, 1.9 fiber, 72mg cholesterol, 357mg sodium, 222mg potassium.

Onion Chicken

Preparation time: 10 min

Cooking time: 45 min

Servings: 4

Ingredients:

- 3 tablespoons olive oil
- 1 cup onion, chopped
- 1-pound chicken breast, skinless, boneless
- ½ teaspoon oregano, dried
- 1 cup of water
- 1 tablespoon parsley, chopped

Directions:

1. Heat a saucepan with 2 tbsp of olive oil over low heat, add the onion, and cook it for 10 minutes.
2. Add all other ingredients except water and cook for another 15 minutes.
3. Then add the water, mix well and cook the chicken for 20 minutes.

Per serving: 232 calories, 24.4g protein, 2.9g carbs, 13.4g fat, 0.7g fiber, 73mg cholesterol, 61mg sodium, 471mg potassium.

Spiced Turkey Fillet

Preparation time: 10 min

Cooking time: 30 min

Servings: 4

Ingredients:

- 2 tablespoons canola oil
- 1 red onion, chopped
- 2 tablespoons oregano
- 1-pound turkey fillet, chopped
- ½ cup of water

Directions:

1. Heat up canola oil in the saucepan.
2. Add turkey, onion, and oregano and cook the ingredients for 5 minutes.
3. Then add water and close the lid.
4. Cook the meal for 25 minutes over medium heat.

Per serving: 187 calories, 24.1g protein, 4g carbs, 7.8g fat, 1.6g fiber, 59mg cholesterol, 259mg sodium, 78mg potassium.

Balsamic Vinegar Chicken

Preparation time: 10 min

Cooking time: 35 min

Servings: 4

Ingredients:

- 1 tablespoon olive oil
- 1-pound chicken breast, skinless, boneless
- 1/3 cup balsamic vinegar
- 2 teaspoons thyme, chopped

- 1 teaspoon rosemary, chopped
- 1 teaspoon lemon zest, grated

Directions:

1. Heat a pan with the oil over medium-high heat, add chicken, cook for 5 minutes, and transfer to a plate.
2. Heat the same tray over medium heat, add all remaining ingredients and bring the mixture to boil.
3. Place the chicken to the saucepan and cook for 10 minutes.
4. Then bake the meal at 325F for 25 minutes.

Per serving: 166 calories, 24.1g protein, 0.8g carbs, 6.4g fat, 0.4g fiber, 73mg cholesterol, 59mg sodium, 443mg potassium.

Citrus Chicken

Preparation time: 10 min

Cooking time: 35 min

Servings: 4

Ingredients:

- 1 tablespoon avocado oil
- 1-pound chicken breast, skinless, boneless, roughly chopped
- 1 orange, chopped
- ½ cup of orange juice
- 1 tablespoon orange zest, grated
- 1 teaspoon ground black pepper
- ½ teaspoon ground turmeric

Directions:

1. Heat a pan with the oil over medium-high heat, add chicken and cook for 5 minutes.
2. Add the rest of the ingredients, toss gently, and bake in the oven at 340°F for 30 minutes.

Per serving: 160 calories, 24.8g protein, 9.7g carbs, 3.5g fat, 1.7g fiber, 73mg cholesterol, 59mg sodium, 593mg potassium.

Glazed Chicken

Preparation time: 10 min

Cooking time: 30 min

Servings: 8

Ingredients:

- 8 chicken thighs, boneless and skinless
- ½ cup balsamic vinegar
- 3 tablespoon garlic, minced
- 1 teaspoon ground black pepper
- 3 tablespoons hot chili sauce

Directions:

1. Put the olive oil in a baking dish, add all ingredients.
2. Toss gently and bake at 425°F for 30 minutes.

Per serving: 275 calories, 42.5g protein, 1.4g carbs, 10.9g fat, 0.2g fiber, 130mg cholesterol, 270mg sodium, 389mg potassium.

Turkey Mushrooms

Preparation time: 10 min

Cooking time: 40 min

Servings: 4

Ingredients:

- 1-pound turkey fillet, sliced
- ½ pound white mushrooms halved
- 1 teaspoon minced garlic
- 2 tablespoons olive oil
- ½ onion, diced
- 1/3 cup water
- 1 tablespoon rosemary, chopped

Directions:

1. Heat a pan with the oil over low-medium heat, add the onions, garlic, and sauté for 5 minutes.
2. Add the remaining ingredients and stir well.
3. Transfer in the preheated to 390°F for 30 minutes.

Per serving: 177 calories, 25.6g protein, 3.9g carbs, 7.8g fat, 1.2g fiber, 59mg cholesterol, 262mg sodium, 211mg potassium.

Spring Chicken Mix

Preparation time: 10 min

Cooking time: 25 min

Servings: 4

Ingredients:

- 1 tablespoon sesame oil
- 1-pound chicken breast, skinless, boneless, chopped
- ½ teaspoon white pepper
- 1 shallot, chopped
- 2 garlic cloves, minced
- 1 cup radish, chopped
- 1 cup spinach, chopped
- 2 cups of water

Directions:

1. Heat olive oil in the saucepan.
2. Add chicken and cook it for 10 minutes.
3. Then add all ingredients, close the lid, and cook for another 15 minutes.

Per serving: 169 calories, 24.6g protein, 2g carbs, 6.3g fat, 0.7g fiber, 73mg cholesterol, 79mg sodium, 540mg potassium.

Peach Turkey

Preparation time: 10 min

Cooking time: 25 min

Servings: 4

Ingredients:

- 1 tablespoon olive oil
- 1 1-pound turkey fillet, chopped
- 1 teaspoon chili powder
- 1 cup peaches, chopped
- 1 teaspoon ground paprika
- 1 cup of water

Directions:

1. Roast the turkey with olive oil in the tray for 5 minutes.
2. Then add all remaining ingredients and stir well.
3. Cook the meal for 20 minutes over medium heat.

Per serving: 144 calories, 27.1g protein, 4.2g carbs, 4.3g fat, 1g fiber, 59mg cholesterol, 264mg sodium, 96mg potassium.

Beef and Pork

Herbs de Provence Pork Chops

Preparation time: 15 min

Cooking time: 14 min

Servings: 4

Ingredients:

- 4 pork top loin chops
- 1 tablespoon herbs de Provence
- 4 teaspoons olive oil

Directions:

1. Rub the pork chops with herbs de Provence and sprinkle with olive oil.
2. After this, preheat the grill to 390F.
3. Pour the pork chops in the grill and roast them for 16 minutes (8 mins per side).

Per serving: 230 calories, 25.9g protein, 0g carbs, 13.6g fat, 0g fiber, 65mg cholesterol, 48mg sodium, 425mg potassium.

Curry Pork Chops

Preparation time: 10 min

Cooking time: 25 min

Servings: 2

Ingredients:

- 2 pork loin chops
- 1 teaspoon curry powder
- ¼ cup of soy milk
- 1 onion, diced
- 1 tablespoon olive oil

Directions:

1. Heat olive oil in the skillet.
2. Then, add pork chops and roast them for 10 minutes (5 minutes per side).
3. Remove the meat from the saucepan and add diced onion. Cook it until the onion is tender.
4. Then add curry powder and soy milk.
5. Bring the mixture to a boil.
6. Add cooked pork chops and cover them in the curry mixture well.
7. Close the lid and cook for 10 minutes over low heat.

Per serving: 341 calories, 19.7g protein, 7.6g carbs, 27.6g fat, 1.7g fiber, 69mg cholesterol, 74mg sodium, 407mg potassium.

Pork Roast with Orange Sauce

Preparation time: 15 min

Cooking time: 80 min

Servings: 4

Ingredients:

- 1-pound pork loin roast
- ½ cup carrot, diced
- ½ cup celery stalk, chopped
- ½ cup onion, diced
- 1 teaspoon Italian seasonings
- 1 cup of orange juice
- 1 tablespoon potato starch

Directions:

1. Then put the celery stalk, carrot and diced onion in the tray.
2. Rub the pork loin with Italian seasonings.
3. Put the meat over the vegetables. Add orange juice.

4. Bake the meat for 75 minutes at 365°F.
5. After this, transfer all vegetables and fluid to the saucepan and bring it to a boil.
6. Shredded the mixture with the blender. Add potato starch and whisk it well.
7. Simmer the sauce for 2 minutes.
8. Cut the cooked meat and drizzle it with orange sauce.

Per serving: 285 calories, 33.2g protein, 12.2g carbs, 11.4g fat, 1g fiber, 93mg cholesterol, 87mg sodium, 704mg potassium.

Southwestern Steak

Preparation time: 15 min

Cooking time: 16 min

Servings: 2

Ingredients:

- 2 beef flank steaks
- 1 tablespoon lemon juice
- 1 teaspoon chili flakes
- 1 teaspoon garlic powder
- 1 tablespoon avocado oil

Directions:

1. Preheat the grill to 385F.
2. Then rub the meat with garlic powder and chili flakes.
3. Then drizzle it with lemon juice and avocado oil.
4. Grill the steaks for 16 minutes (8 minutes per side).

Per serving: 170 calories, 24.2g protein, 1.6g carbs, 6.3g fat, 0.5g fiber, 76mg cholesterol, 58mg sodium, 392mg potassium.

Tender Pork Medallions

Preparation time: 10 min

Cooking time: 25 min

Servings: 3

Ingredients:

- 12 oz pork tenderloin
- 1 teaspoon dried sage
- 1 tablespoon margarine
- 1 teaspoon ground black pepper
- ½ cup low-fat yogurt

Directions:

1. Slice the pork tenderloin into 3 medallions and sprinkle with ground black pepper and sage.
2. Heat margarine in the saucepan and add pork medallions.
3. Roast them for 5 minutes per side.
4. Then add yogurt and cover the meat in it well.
5. Close the lid and cook the medallions for 15 minutes over low-medium heat.

Per serving: 222 calories, 31.4g protein, 3.5g carbs, 8.3g fat, 0.3g fiber, 85mg cholesterol, 138mg sodium, 586mg potassium.

Garlic Pork Meatballs

Preparation time: 10 min

Cooking time: 28 min

Servings: 2

Ingredients:

- 2 pork medallions
- 1 teaspoon minced garlic
- ¼ cup of coconut milk
- 1 tablespoon olive oil
- 1 teaspoon cayenne pepper

Directions:

1. Sprinkle each pork medallion with cayenne pepper.
2. Heat olive oil in the skillet and add meat.
3. Roast the pork medallions for 6 minutes (3 minutes from each side).
4. After this, add minced garlic and coconut milk. Close the lid and cook the meat for 24 mins on low heat.

Per serving: 270 calories, 23.9g protein, 2.6g carbs, 18.8g fat, 0.9g fiber, 70mg cholesterol, 60mg sodium, 103mg potassium.

Fajita Pork Strips

Preparation time: 10 min

Cooking time: 35 min

Servings: 4

Ingredients:

- 16 oz pork sirloin
- 1 tablespoon Fajita seasonings
- 1 tablespoon canola oil

Directions:

1. Slice the pork sirloin into the strips and drizzle with canola oil and fajita seasonings.
2. Then transfer the meat to the baking tray in one layer.
3. Bake it for 36 minutes at 365°F. Stir the meat every 9 minutes during cooking.

Per serving: 180 calories, 18.5g protein, 1.3g carbs, 10.8g fat, 0g fiber, 64mg cholesterol, 157mg sodium, 0mg potassium.

Curry-Rubbed Sirloin with Peanut Dipping Sauce

Preparation time: 30 min

Serving: 8

Ingredients:

Sirloin:

- 1 teaspoon curry powder
- ½ teaspoon ground ginger
- ½ teaspoon granulated garlic
- ½ teaspoon kosher salt
- ½ teaspoon freshly ground black pepper
- Canola oil in a spray pump
- 1¾ pounds sirloin steak, about
- 1-inch thick, excess fat trimmed

Peanut Dipping Sauce:

- ¼ cup smooth peanut butter
- 3 tablespoons brewed cold black tea
- 3 tablespoons light coconut milk
- 2 teaspoons peeled and minced fresh ginger

- 2 teaspoons reduced-sodium soy sauce
- 1½ teaspoons rice vinegar
- 2 teaspoons curry powder
- 1 clove garlic, crushed through a press
- Chopped fresh cilantro or mint for garnish

Directions:

1. Mix the curry powder, ground ginger, granulated garlic, salt, and pepper in a small bowl to prepare the sirloin. Spray the oil with the curry mixture on both sides of the steak and season. Let the peanut sauce stand at room temperature when making it.
2. To make Peanut Dipping Sauce: Mix peanut butter, tea, coconut milk, ginger, soy sauce, vinegar, curry, and garlic in a medium dish.
3. Place a broiler rack about 4 inches from the heat source and preheat to high. Oil the rack for the broiler and add the steak. Broil, turning over the steak after 3 minutes until browned on both sides, and when pressed in the middle, the meat just feels slightly robust, around 6 minutes for medium-rare. Switch to a carving board and quit for 3 minutes to stand.

Sirloin, Shiitake, and Asparagus Stir-Fry

Preparation time: 30 min

Serving: 6

Ingredients:

Sauce:

- ¾ cup Homemade Chicken Broth or canned low-sodium chicken broth
- 2 tablespoons dry sherry or dry vermouth
- 1 tablespoon rice vinegar
- 1 tablespoon low-sodium soy sauce
- 1 tablespoon cornstarch
- ½ teaspoon freshly ground black pepper

Stir fry:

- 4 teaspoons canola oil
- 1-pound sirloin steak, excess fat trimmed, cut across the grain into ¼-inch-thick slices and then into 2-inch strips
- 1 tablespoon peeled and minced fresh ginger
- 2 cloves garlic, minced
- 12 ounces thin asparagus, woody stems discarded, cut into 1-inch lengths
- 6 ounces shiitake mushroom caps, sliced
- 6 ounces sugar snap or snow peas, trimmed
- ½ cup of water
- 3 scallions, white and green parts, cut into 1-inch lengths

Directions:

1. To make the sauce: whisk the broth, sherry, vinegar, soy sauce, corn starch, and pepper together in a small cup.
2. Warm 3 teaspoons of oil in a large nonstick skillet or wok over medium-high heat to stir. Add the steak and cook in two batches, stirring periodically, until seared, for around 2 minutes. Transfer to a dish.
3. In the saucepan, heat the remaining 2 teaspoons of oil over medium to high heat. Apply the ginger and garlic and mix for about 30 seconds until fragrant. Add the snap peas, asparagus, shiitake, and sugar and mix well. Add the water and cook for about 3 minutes, stirring regularly, until the water has evaporated and the vegetables are crisp-tender. Stir in the scallions at the last minute.

Beef and Mushrooms with Sour Cream-Dill Sauce

Preparation time: 30 min

Serving: 4

Ingredients:

- 2 teaspoons canola oil, plus more in a pump sprayer
- 1-pound sirloin steak, excess fat trimmed, cut across the grain in ½-inch-thick slices and then into 2-inch-wide pieces
- 12 ounces cremini mushrooms, sliced
- ¼ cup finely chopped shallots
- 2 teaspoons cornstarch
- ¾ cup Homemade Beef Stock
- ½ cup reduced-fat sour cream
- 1 tablespoon finely chopped fresh dill
- ½ teaspoon kosher salt
- ½ teaspoon freshly ground black pepper

Directions:

1. Spray the wide nonstick skillet over medium-high heat with oil and heat. Attach half of the sirloin and cook until browned on both sides, turning the sirloin pieces halfway through cooking, about 2 minutes. Transfer to a dish. Repeat with the sirloin that remains.
2. Heat 2 teaspoons of oil over low-medium heat in a skillet. Add the mushrooms and cook until the liquid evaporates and they begin to brown, occasionally stirring, for about 6 minutes. Stir in the shallots and cook, around 1 minute, until softened.
3. Sprinkle the cornstarch over the broth in a small bowl and stir to dissolve. Stir the mushrooms and cook until they are thickened. Add the sour cream, dill, salt, and pepper and stir. Return the sirloin and any juices to the skillet on the plate and cook for about 30 seconds until heated. Serve it wet.

Pepper Pork Tenderloins

Preparation time: 15 min

Cooking time: 60 min

Servings: 2

Ingredients:

- 8 oz pork tenderloin
- 1 tablespoon mustard
- 1 teaspoon ground black pepper
- 2 tablespoons olive oil

Directions:

1. Rub the pork with ground black pepper and mustard.
2. Brush it with olive oil and wrap it in the foil.
3. Bake the meat for 60 minutes at 375°F.
4. Then discard the foil and cut the tenderloin into servings.

Per serving: 301 calories, 31.2g protein, 2.6g carbs, 19.6g fat, 1.1g fiber, 83mg cholesterol, 65mg sodium, 529mg potassium.

Spiced Beef

Preparation time: 10 min

Cooking time: 80 min

Servings: 4

Ingredients:

- 1-pound beef sirloin
- 1 tablespoon five-spice seasoning
- 1 bay leaf
- 2 cups of water
- 1 teaspoon peppercorn

Directions:

1. Sprinkle the meat with five-spice seasoning and put it in the saucepan.
2. Add nay leaf, water, and peppercorns.
3. Close the lid and cook it for 1 hour and 20 minutes on medium heat.
4. Chop the cooked meat and rub it with hot spiced water from the saucepan.

Per serving: 203 calories, 34.5g protein, 0.5g carbs, 7.1g fat, 0.2g fiber, 101mg cholesterol, 116mg sodium, 466mg potassium.

Tomato Beef

Preparation time: 10 min

Cooking time: 17 min

Servings: 2

Ingredients:

- 2 chuck shoulder steaks
- ¼ cup tomato sauce
- 1 tablespoon olive oil

1. Brush the steaks with olive oil and tomato sauce and transfer them to the preheated to 390°F grill.
2. Grill the meat for 20 minutes (10 minutes for each side).

Per serving: 240 calories, 20.4g protein, 1.7g carbs, 17.1g fat, 0.5g fiber, 70mg cholesterol, 231mg sodium, 101mg potassium.

Hoisin Pork

Preparation time: 10 min

Cooking time: 14 min

Servings: 4

Ingredients:

- 1-pound pork loin steaks
- 2 tablespoons hoisin sauce
- 1 tablespoon apple cider vinegar
- 1 teaspoon olive oil

Directions:

1. Rub the pork steaks with apple cider vinegar, hoisin sauce and olive oil.
2. Then preheat the grill to 395F.
3. Put the pork in the grill and cook them for 14 minutes (7 minutes per side).

Per serving: 220 calories, 39.3g protein, 3.6g carbs, 10.1g fat, 0.2g fiber, 0mg cholesterol, 130mg sodium, 12mg potassium.

Sage Beef Loin

Preparation time: 10 min

Cooking time: 18 min

Servings: 2

Ingredients:

- 10 oz beef loin, strips
- 1 garlic clove, diced
- 2 tablespoons margarine
- 1 teaspoon dried sage

Directions:

1. Toss margarine in the skillet.
2. Add dried sage, garlic and roast them for 2 minutes on low heat.
3. Add beef and roast them for 16 minutes on medium heat. Mix the meat occasionally.

Per serving: 360 calories, 35.2g protein, 0.8g carbs, 23.2g fat, 0.2g fiber, 101mg cholesterol, 211mg sodium, 497mg potassium.

Spiced Roast Eye of Round

Preparation time: 30 Minutes

Servings: 12

Ingredients:

- 1 teaspoon cumin seeds
- 1 teaspoon coriander seeds
- ½ teaspoon whole black peppercorns
- ½ teaspoon kosher salt
- ½ teaspoon ground ginger
- ¼ teaspoon freshly ground black pepper
- ⅛ teaspoon cayenne pepper
- 1 (3-pound) beef eye of round roast, tied
- 1 clove garlic, cut into about 12 slivers
- Olive oil in a pump sprayer

Directions:

1. In the center of the oven, position a rack and preheat the oven to 400 °F.
2. In a mortar, in an electric spice grinder, or on a work counter under a large skillet, crush the cumin, coriander, and peppercorns together coarsely. Move the salt, ginger, pepper, and cayenne to a dish.
3. Make 1-inch-deep incisions in the beef using the tip of a tiny knife and stuff a garlic clove sliver into each slit. Spray the oil on the beef and sprinkle the spice mixture with it. Place the roast in a roasting pan on a meat rack.
4. For 10 minutes, roast. Reduce the oven's temperature to 350 ° F and proceed to roast until an instant-read thermometer inserted in the beef center reads 125 ° F for a medium-rare duration of about 1 hour. Transfer the beef and let stand for 10 minutes on a carving board.
5. Remove the string and cut it into thin slices with the meat crosswise. Move to a serving dish and pour over the beef with the carving juices. Immediately serve.

Beef Fajitas with Two Peppers

Preparation time: 30 min

Servings: 1

Ingredients:

- 2 teaspoons olive oil, plus more in a pump sprayer

- 1-pound sirloin steak, excess fat trimmed, cut across the grain into ½-inch-thick slices and then into 2-inch-wide pieces
- 12 (8-inch) flour tortillas or Boston lettuce leaves for serving
- 1 green bell pepper, cut into ¼-inch-wide strips
- 1 tablespoon Mexican Seasoning
- 1 red onion, cut into thin half-moons
- 1 large red bell pepper, cut into ¼-inch-wide strips
- 2 cloves garlic, minced
- 12 (8-inch) flour tortillas or Boston lettuce leaves for serving
- Lime wedges for serving.

Directions:

1. Spray the wide nonstick skillet over medium-high heat with oil and heat. Attach half of the sirloin and cook until browned on both sides, turning the sirloin pieces halfway through cooking, about 2 minutes. Transfer to a dish. Repeat with the sirloin that remains.
2. Heat 3 teaspoons of oil over medium-high heat in a skillet. Add the bell peppers, onion, and garlic. Cook for 7 - 10 minutes, occasionally stirring, until tender. Stir in the beef and the Mexican Seasoning with some juices. Move it to a bowl.
3. With the beef mixture fill a flour tortilla or lettuce leaf to serve and squeeze on top with lime juice. Roll up, serve up.

Ground Sirloin and Pinto Chili

Preparation time: 30 min

Servings: 6

Ingredients:

- 1 tablespoon olive oil
- 1 medium yellow onion, chopped
- 2 cloves garlic, minced
- 1¼ pounds ground sirloin
- 1 green bell pepper, cored and chopped
- ½ teaspoon pure ground chipotle chili, or 1 minced canned chipotle chili with its clinging adobo, or ¼ teaspoon cayenne (optional)
- 2 tablespoons chili powder
- ½ teaspoon kosher salt
- 1 (28-ounce) can reduced-sodium chopped tomatoes in juice, undrained
- 2 (15-ounce) cans of reduced-sodium pinto beans, drained and well rinsed

Optional toppings: shredded low-fat Cheddar cheese, nonfat sour cream, chopped fresh cilantro leaves

Directions:

1. Over medium heat, warm the oil in a big saucepan. Attach the onion and bell pepper and cook for about 3 minutes, occasionally stirring, until tender. Add the garlic and cook for another 2 min until it is fragrant. Add the sirloin and cook until it loses its raw appearance, stirring regularly and breaking the meat with the spoon, for around 6 minutes. Add chili powder, ground chipotle (if used), and salt and cook for 1 minute, stirring frequently.
2. Connect the tomatoes and their juice to the mixture and bring to a boil over high heat. Return the heat to medium and simmer for about 15 minutes, stirring periodically, until the juices have thickened slightly. Connect the beans and cook for about 5 minutes, until heated. If you prefer a thicker chili, use a large spoon to mash

some beans into the cooking sauce. Spoon into cups, add the toppings and serve hot if desired.

Beef Chili

Preparation time: 10 min

Cooking time: 30 min

Servings: 4

Ingredients:

- 1 cup lean ground beef
- 1 onion, diced
- 1 tablespoon olive oil
- 1 cup crushed tomatoes
- ½ cup red kidney beans, cooked
- ½ cup of water
- 1 teaspoon chili seasonings

Directions:

1. Heat olive oil in the saucepan and add lean ground beef.
2. Cook it for 7 minutes over medium heat.
3. Then add diced onion and chili seasonings. Mix the ingredients and cook them for 10 mins.
4. After this, add water, red kidney beans, crushed tomatoes and stir the chili well.
5. Close the lid and simmer the meal about for 13 minutes.

Per serving: 202 calories,17.3g protein, 20g carbs, 6.7g fat, 6.1g fiber, 34mg cholesterol, 177mg sodium, 530mg potassium.

Celery Beef Stew

Preparation time: 5 min

Cooking time: 55 min

Servings: 6

Ingredients:

- 1-pound beef loin, chopped
- 2 cups celery stalk, chopped
- 1 garlic clove, diced
- 1 yellow onion, diced
- 1 tablespoon olive oil
- 1 tablespoon tomato paste
- 1 teaspoon chili powder
- 1 teaspoon dried dill
- 2 cups of water

Directions:

1. Cook the beef loin with olive oil in the skillet for 7 minutes.
2. Then, add all ingredients and close the lid.
3. Cook the stew for 50 minutes on low-medium heat,

Per serving: 151 calories,12.6g protein, 3.6g carbs, 7.9g fat, 1.2g fiber, 41mg cholesterol, 370mg sodium, 158mg potassium.

Beef Skillet

Preparation time: 10 min

Cooking time: 30 min

Servings: 3

Ingredients:

- 1 cup lean ground beef
- 1 cup bell pepper, sliced
- 2 tomatoes, chopped

- 1 chili pepper, chopped
- 1 tablespoon olive oil
- ½ cup of water

Directions:

1. Heat olive oil in the skillet and add lean ground beef.
2. Roast it for 10 minutes.
3. Then mix the meat well and add the chili and bell bell pepper. Roast the ingredients for another 10 minutes.
4. Add tomatoes and water.
5. Close the lid and simmer for 10 minutes.

Per serving: 164 calories, 17.1g protein, 6.3g carbs, 8.8g fat, 1.6g fiber, 46mg cholesterol, 50mg sodium, 508mg potassium.

Hot Beef Strips

Preparation time: 10 min

Cooking time: 15 min

Servings: 3

Ingredients:

- 9 oz beef tenders
- 2 tablespoons cayenne pepper
- 1 tablespoon lemon juice
- 2 tablespoons canola oil

Directions:

1. Rub the beef tenders with cayenne pepper and cut into the strips.
2. Drizzle the meat with lemon juice and put it in the hot skillet.
3. Add the oil and roast for 15 minutes over medium heat. Stir occasionally to avoid burning.

Per serving: 231 calories, 22.5g protein, 2.1g carbs, 14.6g fat, 1g fiber, 54mg cholesterol, 62mg sodium, 327mg potassium.

Ground Turkey Fiesta

Preparation time: 10 min

Cooking time: 20 min

Servings: 2

Ingredients:

- ½ cup ground turkey
- ½ cup white beans, cooked
- ½ cup corn kernels, cooked
- 1 tablespoon olive oil
- 1 teaspoon dried rosemary
- 1 teaspoon cayenne pepper
- ½ cup tomato puree

Directions:

1. Put ground turkey in the skillet.
2. Add olive oil, dried rosemary and cayenne pepper.
3. Cook the ingredients for 10 minutes.
4. Then stir them well and add corn kernels, white beans and tomato puree.
5. Cover and cook the meal for 10 minutes on low heat.

Per serving: 330 calories, 25.4g protein, 44.2g carbs, 9.4g fat, 10.4g fiber, 31mg cholesterol, 60mg sodium, 1474mg potassium.

Sloppy Joe

Preparation time: 10 min

Cooking time: 35 min

Servings: 4

Ingredients:

- 1 cup lean ground beef
- 1 cup onion, diced
- ½ cup sweet peppers, diced
- 1 teaspoon minced garlic
- 1 tablespoon canola oil
- 1 teaspoon liquid honey
- ½ cup tomato puree
- 1 teaspoon tomato paste

Directions:

1. Mix up lean ground beef and canola oil in the saucepan.
2. Add sweet pepper and onion, stir the ingredient well.
3. Cook them for 10 minutes.
4. Then add tomato puree, honey and tomato paste. Mix up the mixture well.
5. Cover and cook it for 30 minutes on medium heat.

Per serving: 120 calories, 7.1g protein, 8.2g carbs, 7.7g fat, 1.9g fiber, 22mg cholesterol, 34mg sodium, 170mg potassium.

Beef and Bulgur Meat Loaf

Preparation time: 30 min

Servings: 8

Ingredients:

- 1 cup boiling water ½ cup bulgur
- 2 teaspoons canola oil, plus more in a pump sprayer
- 1 medium yellow onion, chopped
- 1 red bell pepper, cut into ¼-inch dice
- 2 cloves garlic, minced ¼ cup plus
- 2 tablespoons low-salt tomato ketchup
- 1 tablespoon Worcestershire sauce
- 1 teaspoon kosher salt
- ½ teaspoon freshly ground black pepper
- 2 large egg whites
- 1-pound ground sirloin

Directions:

1. Mix the boiling water and bulgur in a heat-resistant medium bowl and leave to stand for around 20 minutes until the bulgur has softened and absorbed the water.
2. Preheat the oven to 350°F meanwhile. Cover with aluminum foil on a rimmed baking sheet and spray with oil.
3. Heat 2 teaspoons of oil over medium heat in a medium nonstick skillet. Add the bell pepper, onion and garlic and cook for about 8 minutes, occasionally stirring, until tender. Transfer and cool slightly in a bowl.
4. In a wire sieve, drain the bulgur, pressing firmly on the bulgur to remove the excess water. Add the vegetables to the bowl, then mix in 1/4 cup of the ketchup, Worcestershire sauce, salt, and pepper. (At this stage, adding these ingredients helps cool the vegetables so that the egg whites don't cook from the heat.) Stir in the whites of the egg. Only add the ground sirloin and blend until mixed. Form the foil-lined baking sheet into an 8 x 4-inch loaf.
5. Bake for 40/50 minutes until the loaf is golden brown and an instant-read thermometer inserted in the center reads 165 °F. Spread the top of the loaf with 2 teaspoons of ketchup over the last minutes.

Beef Ragù with Broccoli Ziti

Preparation time: 30 min

Servings: 6

Ingredients:

- 1 tablespoon olive oil
- 8 ounces ground sirloin
- 1 medium yellow onion, chopped
- 1 medium carrot, cut into ¼-inch dice
- 1 medium celery rib, cut into ¼-inch dice
- 2 cloves garlic, minced
- 1 (28-ounce) can no-salt-added crushed tomatoes
- 2 teaspoons Italian Seasoning
- ¼ teaspoon crushed hot red pepper broccoli Ziti
- 6 tablespoons freshly grated Parmesan cheese

Directions:

1. Heat oil over medium-high heat in a medium saucepan. Add the beef and cook until the meat loses its raw appearance, stirring regularly and breaking the ground sirloin with the spoon, for around 7 minutes. Add the onion, carrot, celery, and garlic and stir. Reduce and cover the heat to medium. Cook, stirring gently, for about 5 minutes, until the vegetables soften.
2. Stir in the onions, hot pepper, and Italian seasoning and bring to a boil. Decrease the heat to low and simmer until the sauce slightly reduces, stirring regularly around 45 minutes.
3. Divide the hot Ziti broccoli into 6 deep bowls. Top each one with the same amount of sauce and, if used, sprinkle with 1 tablespoon of Parmesan cheese. Serve it wet.

Turmeric Meatloaf

Preparation time: 15 min

Cooking time: 50 min

Servings: 6

Ingredients:

- 1 teaspoon ground turmeric
- 1 teaspoon chili flakes
- 2 oz minced onion
- 2 cups lean ground beef
- 2 tablespoons semolina
- 1 tablespoon ketchup
- 1 egg, beaten
- 1 teaspoon olive oil

Directions:

1. Drizzle the meatloaf mold with olive oil.

2. Then, in the mixing bowl, pour all ingredients from the list above.

3. Transfer the meat mixture to the prepared meatloaf and flatten it well.

4. Bake the meatloaf at 375°F for 50/55 minutes.

5. Then cool it well and slice it into servings.

Per serving: 122 calories, 18.5g protein, 3.4g carbs, 5.5g fat, 0.4g fiber, 73mg cholesterol, 82mg sodium, 285mg potassium.

Beef Casserole

Preparation time: 15 min

Cooking time: 45 min

Servings: 5

Ingredients:

- 1 cup zucchini, grated
- 1 teaspoon margarine
- 8 oz lean ground beef
- 1 bell pepper, chopped
- 1 cup tomatoes, crushed
- 1 teaspoon dried thyme
- 1 teaspoon ground black pepper
- 4 oz low-fat feta, crumbled

Directions:

1. Brush the casserole mold with margarine.

2. Mix up dried thyme, ground black pepper and lean ground beef together.

3. Put the mixture in the mold and flatten it well.

4. Top it with bell pepper, zucchini and crumbled low-fat feta.

5. Add crushed tomatoes and cover with foil.

6. Bake the beef casserole in the preheated to 385F oven for 45 minutes.

Per serving: 164 calories,18.9g protein, 5.6g carbs, 8g fat, 1.6g fiber, 8mg cholesterol, 56mg sodium, 379mg potassium.

Garlic Steak

Preparation time: 10 min

Cooking time: 25 min

Servings: 2

Ingredients:

- 2 lean beef steaks
- 1 teaspoon minced garlic
- 1 tablespoon olive oil
- 1 teaspoon apple cider vinegar

Directions:

1. Rub the meat with minced garlic and drizzle with apple cider vinegar.
2. Then heat the skillet well and add olive oil.
3. Add beef steaks and roast them on medium heat for 20 minutes (10 minutes per side).

Per serving: 231 calories,24.9g protein, 0.5g carbs, 12.3g fat, 0g fiber, 76mg cholesterol, 56mg sodium, 350mg potassium.

Ham Casserole

Preparation time: 15 min

Cooking time: 40 min

Servings: 4

Ingredients:

- 8 oz low-sodium ham, chopped
- ¼ cup low-fat yogurt
- 1 teaspoon Italian seasonings
- ½ cup red kidney beans, cooked
- 1 cup spinach, chopped
- ¼ cup low-sodium vegetable broth

Directions:

1. Mix up yogurt and ham. Add Italian seasonings.
2. Transfer the mixture in the casserole mold.
3. Top it with red kidney beans and spinach.
4. Then add broth and cover the casserole with foil.
5. Bake it for 40 minutes at 365°F.

Per serving: 117 calories, 12.1g protein, 16.4g carbs, 1.2g fat, 3.7g fiber, 11mg cholesterol, 197mg sodium, 438mg potassium

Beef Ranch Steak

Preparation time: 10 min

Cooking time: 16 min

Servings: 2

Ingredients:

- 8 oz beef ranch steak (2 servings)
- 1 teaspoon mustard
- 1 tablespoon olive oil
- ½ teaspoon ground nutmeg

Directions:

1. Mix up mustard, ground nutmeg and, olive oil.
2. Then brush the meat with a mustard mixture and transfer it in the preheated to 400F grill.
3. Grill the meat for 16 minutes (8 minutes per side).
4. Then cut the steaks.

Per serving: 460 calories, 23g protein, 35.5g carbs, 25g fat, 4.2g fiber, 0mg cholesterol, 0mg sodium, 13mg potassium.

Pork Casserole

Preparation time: 15 min

Cooking time: 30 min

Servings: 4

Ingredients:

- ¼ cup of rice, cooked
- 10 oz pork loin, chopped
- 4 tomatoes, chopped
- 1 chili pepper, chopped
- ½ tablespoon olive oil

Directions:

1. Roast the pork loin, olive oil and chili pepper in the skillet for 10 minutes.
2. Then transfer the ingredients to the casserole mold.
3. Add rice and chopped tomatoes. Combine the ingredients and cover with foil.
4. Bake the casserole for 20 minutes at 365°F.

Per serving: 231 calories, 22.3g protein, 14.1g carbs, 12g fat, 1.7g fiber, 57mg cholesterol, 51mg sodium, 607mg potassium.

Melted Beef Bites

Preparation time: 10 min

Cooking time: 50 min

Servings: 5

Ingredients:

- 1-pound beef tenderloin, chopped
- 2 cups of water
- 1 teaspoon peppercorns
- 1 teaspoon dried rosemary
- 1 tablespoon tomato paste
- 1 teaspoon margarine

Directions:

1. Put margarine in the saucepan and melt it.

2. Then, add chopped beef and roast it for 5 minutes.
3. After this, add rosemary, peppercorns and tomato paste. Stir well.
4. Add water and close the lid.
5. Cook the meat on low-medium heat for 50 minutes.

Per serving: 160 calories, 27.7g protein, 1g carbs, 6.5g fat, 0.3g fiber, 81mg cholesterol, 75mg sodium, 407mg potassium.

Pork Sliders Meat

Preparation time: 10 min

Cooking time: 60 min

Servings: 3

Ingredients:

- 12 oz pork shoulder roast
- 1 teaspoon ground paprika
- 2 tablespoons ketchup
- 1 teaspoon liquid honey
- 1 teaspoon cayenne pepper
- 1 cup of water
- 1 teaspoon olive oil

Directions:

1. Drizzle olive oil into the saucepan and heat it.
2. Add meat and roast it for 10 minutes (5 minutes per side) until the meat is golden brown from each side.
3. Then add all remaining ingredients and cover.
4. Cook the meat for 50 minutes.
5. When the meat is tender, mince it with the fork.

Per serving: 305 calories, 19.4g protein, 5.2g carbs, 24.9g fat, 0.5g fiber, 80mg cholesterol, 190mg sodium, 69mg potassium.

Beef Saute

Preparation time: 10 min

Cooking time: 47 min

Servings: 2

Ingredients:

- 8 oz beef tenderloin, chopped
- 1 tablespoon avocado oil
- 1 chili pepper, chopped
- 2 bell peppers, chopped
- 1 cup tomatoes, chopped
- ¼ cup of water

Directions:

1. Heat avocado oil in the deep skillet.
2. Add bell pepper, chili pepper and roast the vegetables for 5 minutes.
3. Then stir them well and add beef. Roast the meat for 10 minutes.
4. Add tomatoes and water.
5. Close the lid and sauté the meat for 30 mins on low heat.

Per serving: 258 calories, 33.9g protein, 13.1g carbs, 11.7g fat, 3.1g fiber, 104mg cholesterol, 76mg sodium, 869mg potassium.

Light Shepherd Pie

Preparation time: 15 min

Cooking time: 40 min

Servings: 4

Ingredients:

- 1 cup lean ground beef
- 1 teaspoon tomato paste
- 1 teaspoon chili powder
- ½ cup green peas
- 1 cup potatoes, mashed
- ¼ cup low-fat yogurt
- 1 teaspoon olive oil

Directions:

1. Put lean ground beef in the skillet.
2. Add olive oil and chili powder.
3. Roast the meat for 10 minutes.
4. Then add tomato paste and toss well.
5. After this, transfer the mixture to the casserole mold.
6. Top it with mashed potatoes and green peas.
7. Flatten the potato well.
8. Then sprinkle it with yogurt and cover it with foil.
9. Bake the pie for 30 mins at 375°F.

Per serving: 129 calories, 13.9g protein, 10.2g carbs, 4.5g fat, 2.1g fiber, 35mg cholesterol, 54mg sodium, 435mg potassium.

Meat&Mushrooms Bowl

Preparation time: 10 min

Cooking time: 25 min

Servings: 2

Ingredients:

- 6 oz pork sirloin, sliced
- 1 cup cremini mushrooms, sliced
- 1 tablespoon olive oil
- 1 teaspoon dried dill
- 1 teaspoon ground black pepper
- ½ cup low-fat yogurt

Directions:

1. Roast sliced meat in the saucepan for 5 minutes.
2. Then stir it well and add dill, mushrooms and ground black pepper.
3. Simmler the ingredients for 10 minutes on medium heat.
4. Then, add yogurt and stir the ingredients well.
5. Cover and cook the meal for 10 minutes more.
6. Transfer the cooked meal to the serving bowls.

Per serving: 239 calories, 22.1g protein, 6.8g carbs, 16.2g fat, 0.6g fiber, 57mg cholesterol, 92mg sodium, 334mg potassium.

Tandoori Beef

Preparation time: 15 min

Cooking time: 30 min

Servings: 2

Ingredients:

- 10 oz beef tenderloin, cubed
- 1 teaspoon garam masala
- 2 bell peppers
- 1 tablespoon olive oil
- 1 tablespoon tomato puree
- 1 tablespoon low-fat yogurt

Directions:

1. Mix up yogurt, garam masala and tomato puree.
2. Cover beef cubes in the condiment mixture.
3. String the meat and bell peppers one by one in the skewers.
4. Bake the beef for 30 minutes at 375°F until the meat is tender.

Per serving: 368 calories, 42.8g protein, 10.2g carbs, 20.4g fat, 1.8g fiber, 131mg cholesterol, 96mg sodium, 782mg potassium.

Oregano Pork Tenderloin

Preparation time: 15 min

Cooking time: 60 min

Servings: 4

Ingredients:

- 1-pound pork tenderloin
- 1 tablespoon dried oregano
- 2 tablespoons avocado oil
- 1 teaspoon onion powder
- 1 teaspoon lime zest, grated

Directions:

1. Rub the pork tenderloin with onion powder, dried oregano and lime zest.
2. Then brush it with avocado oil and wrap it in the foil.
3. Bake the meat at 375F for 60 minutes.
4. Slice the cooked meat into servings.

Per serving: 177 calories, 30g protein, 1.7g carbs, 5g fat, 0.9g fiber, 83mg cholesterol, 68mg sodium, 525mg potassium.

Baked Beef Tenders

Preparation time: 15 min

Cooking time: 40 min

Servings: 3

Ingredients:

- 12 oz beef tenderloin
- 1 teaspoon dried rosemary
- 1 onion, chopped
- 1 tablespoon avocado oil

Directions:

1. Chop meat into bite-size pieces and sprinkle with rosemary and avocado oil.
2. Then transfer it to the lined baking sheet. Top the meat with the onion and cover with aluminum foil.
3. Bake the meat for 30 minutes at 365°F.
4. Stir the meat well and cook it without foil for another 10 minutes.

Per serving: 255 calories, 33.3g protein, 3.9g carbs, 11.1g fat, 1.2g fiber, 104mg cholesterol, 69mg sodium, 477mg potassium.

Pork Stuffed Peppers

Preparation time: 15 min

Cooking time: 45 min

Servings: 3

Ingredients:

- 3 bell peppers

- 1 cup lean ground pork
- 1 cup crushed tomatoes with juice
- 1 teaspoon ground black pepper
- 2 tablespoons minced onion
- 1 carrot, grated
- ¼ cup low-fat yogurt

Directions:

1. Mix up lean ground pork, ground black pepper, minced onion, and carrot,
2. Then trim the bell peppers and remove the seeds.
3. Fill the bell peppers with lean ground pork and transfer them to the saucepan.
4. Add crushed tomatoes and yogurt.
5. Close the lid and simmer the meal for 45 minutes on medium-low heat.

Per serving: 394 calories, 31.3g protein, 716.g carbs, 22.2g fat, 5.5g fiber, 99mg cholesterol, 268mg sodium, 717mg potassium.

Fish and Seafood

Spicy Cajun Salmon Bake

Preparation time: 35 min

Servings: 4

Ingredients:

- 1 tablespoon olive oil, plus more in a pump sprayer
- 2 medium Yukon Gold potatoes (8 ounces), scrubbed, unpeeled, and cut into ½-inch-thick slices
- 1 large red bell pepper, cut into ½-inch dice
- 2 celery ribs, coarsely chopped
- 2 cloves garlic, coarsely chopped
- 2 plum tomatoes, seeded and cut into ½-inch dice
- 3 scallions, white and green parts, chopped
- ½ teaspoon kosher salt
- 4 (5-ounce) salmon fillets
- 4 thin lemon slices, plus lemon wedges for serving
- 2 teaspoons Cajun Seasoning

Directions:

1. Preheat the oven to 400F. Spray with oil on a baking dish. Heat 2 tablespoon of oil over medium-high heat in a large nonstick skillet. Attach the potatoes and simmer for about 5 minutes, stirring regularly, before they begin to soften.
2. Add the bell pepper, celery, garlic, and sauté for about 5 more minutes before the pepper softens. Stir in the scallions and tomatoes and sprinkle them with iodine. In the baking bowl, spread.
3. Bake, stirring regularly, for about 25 minutes, until the potatoes are almost tender. Take it out of the microwave. Using the vegetable mixture to arrange the salmon and finish each fillet with a lemon slice. Sprinkle the vegetables and fish with the
4. Seasoning of Cajun. Return to the oven and cook for 8 to 10 minutes until the catfish, when flaked with the tip of the knife, is opaque. Serve hot with wedges of lemon.

Salmon with Grapefruit, Avocado, and Fennel Salad

Preparation time: 35 min

Servings: 4

Ingredients:

Grapefruit, Avocado, and Fennel Salad:

- 1 small fennel bulb
- 2 tablespoons fresh lemon juice
- 1 tablespoon extra-virgin olive oil
- ¼ teaspoon kosher salt
- ¼ teaspoon freshly ground black pepper
- 1 ripe avocado, pitted, peeled, and cut into ½-inch dice
- 1 pink or red grapefruit, peel removed, etched between the membranes into segments

Salmon:

- 2 teaspoons olive oil
- 4 (5-ounce) salmon fillets

Directions:

1. To make the salad: Cut the fennel lengthwise in half. Cut them off if the fronds are attached and lock them. At the base of the bulb, cut out and remove the triangular heart. Break one fennel into small each-moons, each crosswise. Reserve

the remaining half of the fennel and stalks for a different purpose.

2. Whisk the lemon juice and oil together in a medium cup, then season with salt and pepper. Apply the fennel, grapefruit, and avocado and blend gently. Set aside when the cod is being packed.
3. To cook the salmon: Heat the oil over medium heat in a large nonstick skillet. Put in the salmon and protect. Cook until golden on the underside for 3 minutes.
4. Switch and cook, uncovered, changing the heat if required, until golden brown is on the other side of each fillet and the cod looks barely opaque when golden brown is flaked in each fillet, and the cod looks slightly opaque when flaked with the tip of a knife in the middle, about 3 minutes more.
5. Divide the salad with the fennel between four dinner plates. Cover each with a fillet of cod and serve right away.

Rice Paella with Shrimp and Asparagus

Preparation time: 35 min

Servings: 4

Ingredients:

- 8 ounces asparagus, woody stems discarded, cut into 1-inch lengths
- 1 tablespoon olive oil
- 1 medium yellow onion, chopped
- 1 medium red bell pepper, cut into ½-inch dice
- 2 cloves garlic, minced
- 1 cup of rice
- 2 cups Homemade Chicken Broth (here) or canned low-sodium chicken broth
- 1 (14.5-ounce) can no-salt-added diced tomatoes, drained
- ½ cup of water
- 1 teaspoon dried oregano
- ½ teaspoon crushed hot red pepper
- ¼ teaspoon crushed saffron threads
- 8 ounces large shrimp (21 to 25), peeled and deveined
- Lemon wedges, for serving

Directions:

1. Over high heat, put a small saucepan of water to a boil. Attach the asparagus and cook for about 2 minutes, until it's crisp and bright green. (Later on, it will finish cooking.) Drain, clean under running cold water, and then drain again. Only put aside. Heat the oil over low heat in a low Dutch oven or flameproof casserole.
2. Connect the onion, bell pepper, and garlic and simmer for about 3 minutes, stirring periodically, until tender. Stir in the rice, brown. Connect the broth, onions, water, oregano, saffron, and hot pepper, and bring to a boil. Reduce the heat to med-low and cook until the rice has almost completely absorbed the liquid and cook until the rice has almost completely absorbed the liquid, around 40 minutes.
3. Using the Dutch oven to add the shrimp and asparagus. Cover and cook until the entire cod is opaque, about 5 minutes. Remove and uncover from the heat.
4. Let the 3 minutes stand. Serve hot with wedges of lemon.

Limes and Shrimps Skewers

Preparation time: 15 min

Cooking time: 6 min

Servings: 4

Ingredients:

- 1-pound shrimps, peeled
- 1 lime
- 1 teaspoon lemon juice
- ½ teaspoon white pepper

Directions:

1. Cut the lime into wedges.
2. Then drizzle the shrimps with lemon juice and white pepper.
3. Insert shrimp and lime wedges into wooden skewers one by one.
4. Preheat the grill to 400F.
5. Put the skewers on the grill and roast for 6 minutes (3 minutes from each side) until the shrimps become light pink.

Per serving: 132 calories, 26g protein, 3.7g carbs, 2g fat, 0.6g fiber, 239mg cholesterol, 277mg sodium, 214mg potassium.

Crusted Salmon with Horseradish

Preparation time: 10 min

Cooking time: 13 min

Servings: 2

Ingredients:

- 8 oz salmon fillet
- 1 oz horseradish, grated
- ¼ teaspoon ground coriander
- 1 teaspoon coconut flakes
- 1 tablespoon olive oil

Directions:

1. Mix up ground coriander, horseradish, and coconut flakes.
2. Then cut the salmon fillet into 2 servings.
3. Heat olive oil in the skillet.
4. Put the salmon in the skillet and top with the mixture.
5. Cook the fish for 5 minutes on medium heat.
6. Then flip it over and broil for another 8 minutes.

Per serving: 210 calories, 22.2g protein, 1.7g carbs, 14.4g fat, 0.5g fiber, 50mg cholesterol, 95mg sodium, 473mg potassium.

Cucumber and Seafood Bowl

Preparation time: 10 min

Cooking time: 15 min

Servings: 3

Ingredients:

- 2 cucumbers, chopped
- 1 teaspoon mustard
- ½ teaspoon ground coriander
- 1 teaspoon margarine
- 6 oz shrimps, peeled
- 4 oz salmon, chopped
- 1 tablespoon low-fat yogurt

Directions:

1. Heat margarine in the skillet. Add chopped salmon and cook it for 4 minutes (2 min from each side).
2. After this, add shrimps and sprinkle the seafood with ground coriander. Cover and cook the ingredients for 10 minutes on low heat.
3. Then transfer them to the serving bowls. Add cucumbers.
4. Mix up yogurt and mustard.
5. Sprinkle the meal with a mustard mixture.

Per serving: 158 calories, 23.1g protein, 8.9g carbs, 5.2g fat, 1.2g fiber, 136mg cholesterol, 178mg sodium, 557mg potassium.

Fish Tacos

Preparation time: 10 min

Cooking time: 10 min

Servings: 4

Ingredients:

- 4 corn tortillas
- 1 cup white cabbage, shredded
- ¼ cup low-fat yogurt
- 1 teaspoon taco seasonings
- 1-pound cod fillet, chopped
- 1 tablespoon coconut oil

Directions:

1. Sprinkle the chopped cod with taco seasonings.
2. Melt the coconut oil in the skillet.
3. Add cod and cook it until the fish is light brown from each side.
4. Then place the fish on the corn tortillas.
5. Add shredded cabbage.
6. Spread the ingredients with yogurt and wrap in the shape of tacos.

Per serving: 219 calories, 27.5g protein, 13.3g carbs, 5.5g fat, 2g fiber, 70mg cholesterol, 165mg sodium, 110mg potassium.

Tuna and Pineapple Kebob

Preparation time: 10 min

Cooking time: 8 min

Servings: 4

Ingredients:

- 12 oz tuna fillet
- 8 oz pineapple, peeled
- 1 teaspoon olive oil
- ¼ teaspoon ground fennel

Directions:

1. Cut the tuna and pineapple on medium size cubes and sprinkle with olive oil and ground fennel.
2. Then thread them through the skewers and place them in the grill preheated to 400F.
3. Cook the kebobs for 8 minutes (4 minutes per side).

Per serving: 360 calories,19.2g protein, 7.5g carbs, 27.6g fat, 0.8g fiber, 0mg cholesterol, 1mg sodium, 64mg potassium.

Paprika Tilapia

Preparation time: 7 min

Cooking time: 10 min

Servings: 2

Ingredients:

- 2 tilapia fillets
- 1 teaspoon ground paprika
- ½ teaspoon chili powder
- 2 tablespoons avocado oil

Directions:

1. Spread the tilapia fillets with ground paprika and chili powder.
2. Then heat avocado oil in the skillet for 2 minutes.
3. Put the fillets in the hot oil and cook for 6 minutes (3 minutes per side).

Per serving: 1120 calories, 21.4g protein, 1.7g carbs, 3.1g fat, 1.2g fiber, 55mg cholesterol, 47mg sodium, 81mg potassium.

Herbed Sole

Preparation time: 10 min

Cooking time: 10 min

Servings: 3

Ingredients:

- 10 oz sole fillet
- 2 tablespoons margarine
- 1 tablespoon dill weed
- 1 teaspoon garlic powder
- ½ teaspoon cumin seeds

Directions:

1. Toss the margarine in the skillet.
2. Add cumin seeds and dill weed.
3. Dissolve the mixture and simmer for 30 seconds.
4. Then cut the sole fillet into 2 servings and sprinkle with garlic powder.
5. Put the fillets in the melted margarine mixture.
6. Cook the fish for 6 minutes (about 3 minutes per side).

Per serving: 188 calories, 23.3g protein, 1.5g carbs, 9.2g fat, 0.3g fiber, 64mg cholesterol, 191mg sodium, 380mg potassium.

Shrimp Tacos with Lime-Cilantro Slaw

Preparation time: 35 min

Servings: 4

Ingredients:

Shrimp:

- 2 tablespoons fresh lime juice
- 2 teaspoons chili powder
- 1½ pounds shrimps

Slaw:

- 2 scallions, white & green parts, finely chopped
- 2 tablespoons fresh lime juice
- 2 tablespoons finely chopped fresh cilantro
- Freshly grated zest of 1 lime
- 2 tablespoons light mayonnaise
- 1 (12-ounce) bag coleslaw mix
- ½ teaspoon kosher salt
- 2 plum (Roma) tomatoes, cut into ½-inch dice

- Olive oil in a pump sprayer
- 12 (6-inch) corn tortillas, warmed Lime wedges, for serving

Directions:

1. To cook the fish: Whisk the lime juice and chili powder together in a small glass or ceramic baking dish. Marinate the shrimps. When making the slaw, cover and refrigerate.
2. Whisk together the lime zest, juice, and mayonnaise in a big bowl to make the slaw. Apply the combination of coleslaw, onions, cilantro, scallions, and salt and blend well. Only put aside. Mix well. Only put aside.
3. Spray the wide nonstick skillet over medium-high heat with oil and heat. Remove the fish from the baking dish and let it drain back into the jar with the excess liquid.
4. Place in the skillet and cook for around 8 minutes, turning regularly. Switch to a serving bowl and flake with a fork into large chunks.
5. Spoon some shrimps and slaw onto a tortilla with each meal, then fold and enjoy with a drizzle of lime-juice if you like.

Rosemary Salmon

Preparation time: 10 min

Cooking time: 12 min

Servings: 4

Ingredients:

- 1-pound salmon fillet
- 4 teaspoons olive oil
- 4 teaspoons lemon juice
- 1 tablespoon dried rosemary

Directions:

1. Cut the salmon fillet into 4 servings.
2. Then spread the fillets with olive oil, lemon juice, and dried rosemary.
3. Put the salmon on the pan and bake it for 12 minutes at 400°F.

Per serving: 190 calories, 22.1g protein, 0.6g carbs, 11.8g fat, 0.4g fiber, 50mg cholesterol, 51mg sodium, 450mg potassium.

Tuna Stuffed Zucchini Boats

Preparation time: 15 min

Cooking time: 20 min

Servings: 2

Ingredients:

- 1 zucchini, trimmed
- 6 oz tuna, canned
- 2 oz low-fat cheese, shredded
- 1 teaspoon chili flakes
- 1 teaspoon olive oil

Directions:

1. Chop zucchini in half and scoop out zucchini pulp to make zucchini boats.
2. Fill the zucchini boats with shredded cheese and tuna.
3. Drizzle the zucchini with olive oil and transfer it in the oven.
4. Cook the meal at 385°F for 20 minutes.

Per serving: 318 calories, 30.8g protein, 3.7g carbs, 18.8g fat, 1.1g fiber, 56mg cholesterol, 229mg sodium, 570mg potassium.

Baked Cod

Preparation time: 10 min

Cooking time: 30 min

Servings: 2

Directions:

- 10 oz cod fillet
- 1 teaspoon Italian seasonings
- 1 tablespoon margarine

Ingredients:

1. Rub the baking pan with margarine.
2. Then chop the cod and rub with Italian seasonings.
3. Put the fish in the tray and cover with foil.
4. Bake the meal at 375°F for 30 minutes.

Per serving: 180 calories, 26.1g protein, 0.3g carbs, 7.6g fat, 0g fiber, 70mg cholesterol, 155mg sodium, 4mg potassium.

Basil Halibut

Preparation time: 10 min

Cooking time: 10 min

Servings: 4

Ingredients:

- 1-pound halibut, chopped
- 1 tablespoon dried basil
- 1 teaspoon garlic powder
- 2 tablespoons olive oil

Directions:

1. Put olive oil into the saucepan and heat it.
2. Meanwhile, mix up halibut, garlic powder and dried basil.
3. Mix the fish in the hot oil and coot it for about 6 minutes (3 minutes per side).

Per serving: 337 calories, 22.1g protein, 0.5g carbs, 28.2g fat, 0.1g fiber, 70mg cholesterol, 123mg sodium, 420mg potassium.

Tilapia Veracruz

Preparation time: 10 min

Cooking time: 20 min

Servings: 4

Ingredients:

- 1 cup tomatoes, chopped
- 1 teaspoon dried oregano
- 1 onion, diced
- ½ cup bell pepper, chopped
- ¼ cup of water
- 1 tablespoon olive oil
- 4 tilapia fillets

Directions:

1. Heat olive oil in the skillet and add tilapia fillets.
2. Broil the fish for 4 minutes per side. Remove the fish from the skillet.
3. Then, add the onion to the casserole and cook it for 2 minutes.
4. Add bell peppers, tomatoes and oregano. Toss the ingredients well and cook them for 5 minutes.
5. After this, add water and fish.

6. Cover and cook the meal for another 5 minutes.

Per serving: 128 calories, 21.9g protein, 5.7g carbs, 4.7g fat, 1.5g fiber, 55mg cholesterol, 44mg sodium, 181mg potassium.

Lemon Swordfish

Preparation time: 10 min

Cooking time: 25 min

Servings: 4

Ingredients:

- 18 oz swordfish fillets
- 1 tablespoon margarine
- 1 teaspoon lemon zest
- 3 tablespoons lemon juice
- 1 teaspoon ground black pepper
- 2 tablespoons olive oil
- ½ teaspoon minced garlic

Directions:

1. Cut the fish into 4 servings.
2. After this, mix up lemon zest, lemon juice, ground black pepper, and olive oil in the mixing bowl. Add minced garlic.
3. Rub the fish fillets with lemon mixture.
4. Brush the baking pan with margarine and arrange the swordfish fillets.
5. Cook the fish for 25 minutes at 390°F.

Per serving: 278 calories, 32.6g protein, 0.8g carbs, 16.5g fat, 0.2g fiber, 64mg cholesterol, 183mg sodium, 496mg potassium.

Spiced Scallops

Preparation time: 10 min

Cooking time: 5 min

Servings: 4

Ingredients:

- 1-pound scallops
- 1 teaspoon Cajun seasonings
- 1 tablespoon olive oil

Directions:

1. Rub the scallops with Cajun seasonings.
2. Heat olive oil in the skillet.
3. Then, add scallops and cook them for 2 minutes per side.

Per serving: 140 calories, 19g protein, 2.7g carbs, 4.4g fat, 0g fiber, 37mg cholesterol, 195mg sodium, 365mg potassium

Shrimp Putanesca

Preparation time: 5 min

Cooking time: 20 min

Servings: 3

Ingredients:

- 5 oz shrimps, peeled
- 1 teaspoon chili flakes
- ½ onion, diced
- 1 tablespoon coconut oil
- 1 teaspoon garlic, diced
- 1 cup tomatoes, chopped
- ¼ cup olives, sliced
- ¼ cup of water

Directions:

1. Heat coconut oil in the saucepan.
2. Add shrimps and chili flakes. Cook the shrimps for 4 minutes.
3. Toss them well and add diced onion, garlic, tomatoes, water and olives.
4. Cover and sauté the meal for 15 minutes.

Per serving: 118 calories,10.7g protein, 5.8g carbs, 6.7g fat, 1.5g fiber, 100mg cholesterol, 217mg sodium, 255mg potassium.

Curry Snapper

Preparation time: 10 min

Cooking time: 15 min

Servings: 4

Ingredients:

- 1-pound snapper fillet, chopped
- 1 teaspoon curry powder
- 1 cup celery stalk, chopped
- ½ cup low-fat yogurt
- ¼ cup of water
- 1 tablespoon olive oil

Directions:

1. Broil the snapper fillet in the olive oil for 4 minutes (2 per side).
2. Then, add celery stalk, low-fat yogurt, curry powder and water.
3. Toss the fish until you get the homogenous texture.
4. Close the lid and cook the fish for 10 minutes on low-medium heat.

Per serving: 200 calories,28.5g protein, 3.2g carbs, 5.9g fat, 0.6g fiber, 52mg cholesterol, 105mg sodium, 145mg potassium.

Grouper with Tomato Sauce

Preparation time: 10 min

Cooking time: 15 min

Servings: 2

Ingredients:

- 12 oz grouper, chopped
- 2 cups grape tomatoes, chopped
- 1 chili pepper, chopped
- 1 tablespoon margarine
- 1 teaspoon ground coriander

Directions:

1. Toss the margarine in the saucepan.
2. Then, add chopped grouper and sprinkle it with ground coriander.
3. Broil the fish for 2 minutes per side.
4. Then add grape tomatoes and chili pepper.
5. Toss the ingredients well and close the lid.
6. Cook the fish for 10 minutes on low heat.

Per serving: 295 calories,43.9g protein, 7.2g carbs, 8.3g fat, 2.2g fiber, 80mg cholesterol, 166mg sodium, 1243mg potassium.

Braised Seabass

Preparation time: 8 min

Cooking time: 28 min

Servings: 2

Ingredients:

- 10 oz seabass fillet
- 1 cup tomatoes, chopped
- 1 yellow onion, sliced
- 1 tablespoon avocado oil
- 1 teaspoon ground black pepper

Directions:

1. Heat olive oil in the skillet.
2. Add seabass fillet and broil it for 4 minutes per side.
3. Then remove the fish from the casserole and add sliced onion.
4. Cook it for 2 minutes.
5. After this, add ground black pepper and tomatoes.
6. Bring the mixture to a boil.
7. Add cooked seabass and close the lid.
8. Cook the fillet for 15 minutes.

Per serving: 265 calories, 29.7g protein, 9.7g carbs, 15.3g fat, 3.8g fiber, 0mg cholesterol, 8mg sodium, 329mg potassium.

Five-Spices Sole

Preparation time: 10 min

Cooking time: 11 min

Servings: 3

Ingredients:

- 3 sole fillets
- 1 tablespoon five-spice seasonings
- 1 tablespoon coconut oil

Directions:

1. Rub the sole fillets with seasonings.
2. Then heat the coconut oil in the saucepan for 2 minutes.
3. Put the sole fillets in the hot oil and cook them for 10 minutes (5 minutes per side).

Per serving: 224 calories, 30.8g protein, 1g carbs, 6.5g fat, 2.2g fiber, 86mg cholesterol, 133mg sodium, 437mg potassium.

Clams Stew

Preparation time: 8 min

Cooking time: 10 min

Servings: 5

Ingredients:

- 1-pound clams
- 1 teaspoon dried thyme
- 1 teaspoon ground paprika
- ½ cup light cream (low-fat)
- 1 tablespoon lemon juice

Directions:

1. Put dried thyme, ground paprika, and cream.
2. Bring the liquid to a boil.
3. Then squeeze lemon juice and whisk the mixture well.
4. Add clams and close the lid.
5. Cook the clams stew for 6 minutes.

Per serving: 95 calories, 0.6g protein, 12g carbs, 5.1g fat, 0.6g fiber, 16mg cholesterol, 345mg sodium, 96mg potassium

Salmon in Capers

Preparation time: 10 min

Cooking time: 15 min

Servings: 4

Ingredients:

- 2 tablespoons avocado oil
- 1-pound salmon fillet, chopped
- 1 tablespoon capers, drained
- ½ cup low-fat milk

Directions:

1. Heat a pan with the oil over medium-high heat, add salmon and roast it for 5 minutes.
2. Add milk and capers and sautèe the meal for 10 minutes over medium heat.

Per serving: 163 calories, 23.2g protein, 2g carbs, 8.2g fat, 0.4g fiber, 52mg cholesterol, 127mg sodium, 504mg potassium

Mustard Tuna Salad

Preparation time: 10 min

Cooking time: 0 min

Servings: 2

Ingredients:

- ¼ teaspoon cayenne pepper
- ½ teaspoon lemon juice
- ¼ cup chickpeas, cooked
- 1 tablespoon mustard
- 5 ounces white tuna canned, drained
- 1 teaspoon olive oil

Directions:

1. Mix up olive oil, lemon juice and mustard in the shallow bowl.
2. Pour all remaining ingredients in the salad bowl and top with mustard. Toss the salad well.

Per serving: 209 calories, 23g protein, 17.3g carbs, 7.6g fat, 5.2g fiber, 30mg cholesterol, 274mg sodium, 431mg potassium

Shallot Tuna

Preparation time: 10 min

Cooking time: 10 min

Servings: 4

Ingredients:

- 1-pound tuna fillet, chopped
- 1 tablespoon olive oil
- ½ cup shallot, chopped
- 2 tablespoons lime juice
- ½ cup of water

Directions:

1. Heat a pan with the oil over medium-high heat, add shallots and sauté for 3 minutes.
2. Then, add the fish and cook it for about 8 minutes (4 on each side).
3. Then drizzle the fish with lime juice and water.
4. Cover and simmer the tuna for 3 minutes.

Per serving: 448 calories, 25.3g protein, 3.9g carbs, 38.7g fat, 0g fiber, 0mg cholesterol, 5mg sodium, 73mg potassium

Cod Relish

Preparation time: 10 min

Cooking time: 5 min

Servings: 4

Ingredients:

- 1 teaspoon dried oregano
- 1 cup green peas, cooked
- 1 onion, diced
- 3 tablespoons olive oil
- ½ teaspoon white pepper
- 1-pound cod fillet, chopped

Directions:

1. Heat a pan with 1 tablespoon oil over medium-high heat, add the cod fillets, cook it for 2 minutes on each side.
2. After this, put the fish on the serving plates.
3. In the mixing bowl, mix up all remaining ingredients and shale well.
4. Top the fish with an onion mixture.

Per serving: 223 calories, 22.6g protein, 8.2g carbs, 11.7g fat, 2.7g fiber, 56mg cholesterol, 74mg sodium, 138mg potassium

Mint Cod

Preparation time: 10 min

Cooking time: 7 min

Servings: 4

Ingredients:

- 1 tablespoon avocado oil
- 1 tablespoon lemon juice
- 1 tablespoon mint, chopped 1-pound cod fillet
- 2 tablespoons water

Directions:

1. Heat a tray with the oil over medium heat, add mint and cod.
2. Cook the fish for 3 minutes per side.
3. Then add water and lemon juice. Cook the cod for 2 minutes more.

Per serving: 97 calories, 20.4g protein, 0.4g carbs, 1.5g fat, 0.3g fiber, 56mg cholesterol, 72mg sodium, 22mg potassium

Dill Steamed Salmon

Preparation time: 10 min

Cooking time: 0 min

Servings: 4

Ingredients:

- 2 tablespoons dill, chopped
- 1 tablespoon low-fat cream cheese
- 1 teaspoon chili flakes
- 1-pound steamed salmon, chopped
- 1 red onion, diced

Directions:

1. Mix up all ingredients in the bowl and carefully stir until homogenous.

Per serving: 174 calories, 22.8g protein, 3.5g carbs, 8g fat, 0.8g fiber, 53mg cholesterol, 62mg sodium, 531mg potassium

Cod in Tomatoes

Preparation time: 10 min

Cooking time: 16 min

Servings: 4

Ingredients:

- 2 tablespoons avocado oil
- ½ teaspoon minced garlic
- ½ cup of water
- 4 cod fillets, boneless
- 1 cup plum tomatoes, chopped
- 1 teaspoon scallions, chopped

Directions:

1. Heat a pan with the oil over medium-high heat, add the garlic and the fish and cook for 3 minutes per side.
2. Then top the fish with the remaining ingredients and cook for 10 minutes more.

Per serving: 110 calories, 20.7g protein, 2.9g carbs, 2g fat, 0.8g fiber, 40mg cholesterol, 87mg sodium, 117mg potassium

Spinach Halibut

Preparation time: 10 min

Cooking time: 6 min

Servings: 4

Ingredients:

- 4 halibut fillets
- 2 tablespoons spinach, blended
- 1 teaspoon margarine

Directions:

1. Melt the margarine in the skillet and add fish fillets.
2. Cook them for 3 minutes per side.
3. Top the cooked halibut with spinach.

Per serving: 327 calories, 60.5g protein, 0g carbs, 7.7g fat, 0g fiber, 93mg cholesterol, 168mg sodium, 1312mg potassium

Paprika Tuna Steaks

Preparation time: 10 min

Cooking time: 4 min

Servings: 4

Ingredients:

- 1 teaspoon avocado oil
- 4 tuna steaks, boneless
- 1 teaspoon ground paprika

Directions:

1. Rub the fish with paprika and sprinkle with avocado oil.
2. Then transfer the tuna steaks in the preheated to 400F grill and cook for 2 minutes per side.

Per serving: 159 calories, 25.5g protein, 0.4g carbs, 5.6g fat, 0.3g fiber, 42mg cholesterol, 43mg sodium, 291mg potassium

Grilled Tilapia

Preparation time: 10 min

Cooking time: 6 min

Servings: 4

Ingredients:

- 1 tablespoon sesame oil
- ½ teaspoon ground black pepper
- ½ teaspoon garlic powder
- 4 medium tilapia fillets

Directions:

1. Sprinkle the fish with garlic powder, ground black pepper, and sesame oil.
2. Grill it for 3 minutes per side in the preheated to 400F grill.

Per serving: 125 calories, 21.1g protein, 0.4g carbs, 4.4g fat, 0.1g fiber, 55mg cholesterol, 40mg sodium, 7mg potassium

Cod in Orange Juice

Preparation time: 5 min

Cooking time: 12 min

Servings: 4

Ingredients:

- 4 cod fillets, boneless
- 1 cup of orange juice
- 1 tablespoon chives, chopped
- 1 tablespoon olive oil
- ½ teaspoon white pepper

Directions:

1. Heat a saucepan with the oil over medium heat.
2. Sprinkle the fish with white pepper and out in the hot oil.
3. Add orange juice and chives.
4. Cook the fish for 10 minutes.

Per serving: 149 calories, 20.5g protein, 6.7g carbs, 4.7g fat, 0.2g fiber, 40mg cholesterol, 81mg sodium, 129mg potassium

Tomato Halibut Fillets

Preparation time: 10 min

Cooking time: 10 min

Servings: 4

Ingredients:

- 2 teaspoon sesame oil
- 4 halibut fillets, skinless
- 1 cup cherry tomatoes, halved
- 1 teaspoon dried basil

Directions:

1. Sprinkle the fish with basil and put it in the hot skillet.
2. Add sesame oil and cherry tomatoes.
3. Roast the meal for 4 minutes and then stir well and cook for 5 minutes more.

Per serving: 346 calories, 60.9g protein, 1.8g carbs, 9.1g fat, 0.5g fiber, 93mg cholesterol, 158mg sodium, 1414mg potassium

Salmon with Basil and Garlic

Preparation time: 5 min

Cooking time: 14 min

Servings: 4

Ingredients:

- 2 tablespoons avocado oil
- 4 salmon fillets, skinless
- 1 teaspoon dried basil
- ½ teaspoon garlic powder

Directions:

1. Heat a large-skillet with the olive oil, add the fish and cook for 4 minutes per side.
2. Sprinkle the cooked salmon with garlic powder and basil.

Per serving: 246 calories, 34.7g protein, 0.7g carbs, 11.9g fat, 0.3g fiber, 78mg cholesterol, 79mg sodium, 710mg potassium

Mustard Arctic Char

Preparation time: 10 min

Cooking time: 10 min

Servings: 2

Ingredients:

- 1 tablespoon mustard
- 1 tablespoon olive oil
- ¼ teaspoon dried rosemary
- 2 arctic char fillets

Directions:

1. Sprinkle the fish with rosemary, olive oil, and mustard.
2. Then transfer the fish fillets in the baking pan and bake for 10 at 400F.

Per serving: 291 calories, 25.4g protein, 2.1g carbs, 10.6g fat, 0.9g fiber, 8mg cholesterol, 22mg sodium, 40mg potassium

Cod in Yogurt Sauce

Preparation time: 10 min

Cooking time: 15 min

Servings: 4

Ingredients:

- 1 teaspoon sesame oil
- 4 cod fillets, boneless and skinless
- ½ onion, diced
- ½ cup low-fat yogurt
- 1 tablespoon dried cilantro
- ½ teaspoon minced garlic

Directions:

1. Rub the cod fillets with dried cilantro, minced garlic, and sesame oil.
2. Put the fish in the casserole and cook it for 3 minutes per side.
3. Add onion and fat yogurt. Cook the meal for 12 minutes more.

Per serving: 128 calories, 21.9g protein, 3.6g carbs, 2.5g fat, 0.3g fiber, 42mg cholesterol, 102mg sodium, 94mg potassium

Parsley Trout

Preparation time: 10 min

Cooking time: 10 min

Servings: 6

Ingredients:

- 1 tablespoon dried parsley

- 6 trout fillets
- 2 tablespoons margarine

Directions:

1. Rub the trout fillets with parsley.
2. Then toss the margarine in the skillet and melt it.
3. Add fish fillets and cook them for 4 minutes per side.

Per serving: 152 calories,16.6g protein, 0.1g carbs, 9g fat, 0g fiber, 46mg cholesterol, 86mg sodium, 293mg potassium

Vegan and Vegetarian

Mushroom Florentine

Preparation time: 10 min

Cooking time: 20 min

Servings: 4

Ingredients:

- 5 oz whole-grain pasta
- ¼ cup low-sodium vegetable broth
- 1 cup mushrooms, sliced
- ¼ cup of soy milk
- 1 teaspoon olive oil
- ½ teaspoon Italian seasonings

Directions:

1. Cook the pasta following the directions on the product.
2. Then pour olive oil into the saucepan and heat it.
3. Add Italian seasonings and mushrooms. Toss the mushrooms well and cook for 10 minutes.
4. Then add soy milk and vegetable broth.
5. Add cooked pasta and stir the mixture well. Cook it for 7 minutes on low heat.

Per serving: 297 calories, 14.4g protein, 50.4g carbs, 4.2g fat, 9g fiber, 0mg cholesterol, 26mg sodium, 74mg potassium.

Bean Hummus

Preparation time: 10 min

Cooking time: 40 min

Servings: 6

Ingredients:

- 1 cup chickpeas, soaked
- 6 cups of water
- 1 tablespoon tahini paste
- 2 garlic cloves,
- ¼ cup olive oil
- ¼ cup lemon juice
- 1 teaspoon harissa

Directions:

1. Pour water into the saucepan. Add chickpeas and close the lid.
2. Cook the chickpeas for 40 minutes on low heat or until they are soft.
3. After this, transfer the cooked chickpeas to the food processor.
4. Add olive oil, harissa, lemon juice, garlic cloves, and tahini paste.
5. Blend the hummus until it is smooth.

Per serving: 205 calories, 7.1g protein, 21.6g carbs, 12g fat, 6.1g fiber, 0mg cholesterol, 30mg sodium, 321mg potassium.

Hasselback Eggplant

Preparation time: 15 min

Cooking time: 25 min

Servings: 2

Ingredients:

- 2 eggplants, trimmed
- 2 tomatoes, sliced
- 1 tablespoon low-fat yogurt
- 1 teaspoon curry powder
- 1 teaspoon olive oil

Directions:

1. Make the cuts in the eggplant in the shape of Hasselback.
2. Then spread the vegetables with curry powder and fill with sliced tomatoes.
3. Drizzle the eggplants with olive oil and yogurt and wrap them in the foil (each Hasselback eggplant wrap separately).
4. Bake the vegetables at 375°F for 25 minutes.

Per serving: 190 calories, 8g protein, 38.1g carbs, 3g fat, 21.2g fiber, 0mg cholesterol, 23mg sodium, 1580mg potassium.

Vegetarian Kebabs

Preparation time: 10 min

Cooking time: 6 min

Servings: 4

Ingredients:

- 2 tablespoons balsamic vinegar
- 1 tablespoon olive oil
- 1 teaspoon dried parsley
- 2 tablespoons water
- 2 sweet peppers
- 2 red onions, peeled
- 2 zucchinis, trimmed

Directions:

1. Cut the sweet peppers and onions into medium-sized squares.
2. Then slice the zucchini.
3. String all vegetables into the skewers.
4. After this, mix up olive oil, dried parsley, water, and balsamic vinegar in the shallow bowl.
5. Drizzle the vegetable skewers with olive oil mixture and transfer to the preheated to 390F grill.
6. Cook the kebabs for about 6 minutes (3 minutes per side).

Per serving: 89 calories, 2.8g protein, 13g carbs, 3.9g fat, 3.1g fiber, 0mg cholesterol, 14mg sodium, 456mg potassium

White Beans Stew

Preparation time: 10 min

Cooking time: 55 min

Servings: 4

Ingredients:

- 1 cup white beans, soaked
- 1 cup low-sodium vegetable broth
- 1 cup zucchini, chopped
- 1 teaspoon tomato paste
- 1 tablespoon avocado oil
- 4 cups of water
- ½ teaspoon peppercorns
- ½ teaspoon ground black pepper
- ¼ teaspoon ground nutmeg

Directions:

1. Heat avocado oil in the saucepan, add zucchinis and roast them for 5 minutes.
2. After this, add white beans, vegetable broth, tomato paste, water, peppercorns, ground black pepper, and ground nutmeg.
3. Cover and simmer the stew for 50 minutes on low heat.

Per serving: 184 calories, 12.3g protein, 32.6g carbs, 1g fat, 8.3g fiber, 0mg cholesterol, 55mg sodium, 1011mg potassium.

Vegetarian Lasagna

Preparation time: 10 min

Cooking time: 30 mi

Servings: 6

Ingredients:

- 1 cup carrot, diced
- ½ cup bell pepper, diced
- 1 cup spinach, chopped
- 1 tablespoon olive oil
- 1 teaspoon chili powder
- 1 cup tomatoes, chopped
- 4 oz low-fat cottage cheese
- 1 eggplant, sliced
- 1 cup low-sodium vegetable broth

Directions:

1. Put bell pepper, carrot and spinach in the saucepan.
2. Add chili powder, olive oil and stir the vegetables well. Cook them for 5 minutes.
3. After this, make the layer of sliced eggplant in the casserole mold and cover it with vegetable mixture.
4. Add tomatoes, vegetable stock and cottage cheese.
5. Bake the lasagna for 30 minutes at 375°F.

Per serving: 80 calories, 4.1g protein, 9.7g carbs, 3g fat, 3.9g fiber, 2mg cholesterol, 124mg sodium, 377mg potassium.

Carrot Cakes

Preparation time: 10 min

Cooking time: 10 min

Servings: 4

Ingredients:

- 1 cup carrot, grated
- 1 tablespoon semolina
- 1 egg, beaten
- 1 teaspoon Italian seasonings
- 1 tablespoon sesame oil

Directions:

1. In the bowl, mix up grated carrot, semolina, egg, and Italian seasonings.
2. Heat sesame oil in the skillet.
3. Make the carrot cakes with 2 spoons and put them in the skillet.
4. Cook the cakes for 4 minutes per side.

Per serving: 72 calories, 1.9g protein, 4.8g carbs, 4.9g fat, 0.8g fiber, 42mg cholesterol, 35mg sodium, 108mg potassium.

Vegan Chili

Preparation time: 10 min

Cooking time: 25 min

Servings: 4

Ingredients:

- ½ cup bulgur
- 1 cup tomatoes, chopped
- 1 chili pepper, chopped
- 1 cup red kidney beans, cooked
- 2 cups low-sodium vegetable broth
- 1 teaspoon tomato paste
- ½ cup celery stalk, chopped

Directions:

1. Put all ingredients in the big skillet and stir well.
2. Cover and simmer the chili for 25 minutes over medium-low heat.

Per serving: 234 calories,13.1g protein, 44.9g carbs, 0.9g fat, 11g fiber, 0mg cholesterol, 92mg sodium, 852mg potassium.

Aromatic Whole Grain Spaghetti

Preparation time: 5 min

Cooking time: 10 min

Servings: 2

Ingredients:

- 1 teaspoon dried basil
- ¼ cup of soy milk
- 6 oz whole-grain spaghetti
- 2 cups of water
- 1 teaspoon ground nutmeg

Directions:

1. Bring the water to boil, then add spaghetti and cook them for 8-10 minutes.
2. Meanwhile, bring the soy milk to boil.
3. Drain the cooked pasta and mix them up with ground nutmeg, soy milk and dried basil.
4. Stir the meal well.

Per serving: 122 calories,6.6g protein, 25g carbs, 1.4g fat, 4.3g fiber, 0mg cholesterol, 25mg sodium, 81mg potassium.

Chunky Tomatoes

Preparation time: 5 min

Cooking time: 15 min

Servings: 3

Ingredients:

- 2 cups plum tomatoes, roughly chopped
- ½ cup onion, diced
- ½ teaspoon garlic, diced
- 1 teaspoon Italian seasonings
- 1 teaspoon canola oil
- 1 chili pepper, chopped

Directions:

1. Heat canola oil in the saucepan.
2. Add chili pepper and onion. Cook the vegetables for 5 minutes. Stir them from time to time.
3. Then, add tomatoes, garlic, and Italian seasonings.
4. Cover and sauté the meal for 10 minutes.

Per serving: 450 calories,1.7g protein, 8.4g carbs, 2.3g fat, 1.8g fiber, 1mg cholesterol, 17mg sodium, 279mg potassium.

Baby minted carrots

Preparation time: 35 min

Servings: 6

Ingredients:

- 6 cups of water
- 1-pound baby carrots, rinsed (about 5 1/2 cups)

- 1/4 cup 100% apple juice
- 1 tablespoon cornstarch
- 1/2 tablespoon chopped fresh mint leaves
- 1/8 teaspoon ground cinnamon

Directions:

1. Through a large bowl, pour the water. Add the carrots and simmer for about 10 minutes, until tender-crisp. Drain the carrots in a serving bowl and set them aside.
2. Combine the apple juice and cornstarch in a shallow saucepan over moderate heat. Stir for about 5 minutes before the mixture thickens. Stir in the cinnamon and mint.
3. Pour over the carrots with the combination. Immediately serve.

Baked Falafel

Preparation time: 10 min

Cooking time: 25 min

Servings: 6

Ingredients:

- 2 cups chickpeas, cooked
- 1 yellow onion, diced
- 3 tablespoons olive oil
- 1 cup fresh parsley, chopped
- 1 teaspoon ground cumin
- ½ teaspoon coriander
- 2 garlic cloves, diced

Directions:

1. Pour all ingredients in the blender and blend until smooth.
2. Preheat the oven to 375F.
3. Then line the baking sheet with baking paper.
4. Make balls with the chickpea mixture and gently press them into a falafel shape.
5. Put the falafel in the pan and bake in the oven for 25 minutes.

Per serving: 326 calories, 13.5g protein, 43.3g carbs, 11.2g fat, 12.4g fiber, 0mg cholesterol, 23mg sodium, 676mg potassium.

Paella

Preparation time: 10 min

Cooking time: 25 min

Servings: 6

Ingredients:

- 1 teaspoon dried saffron
- 1 cup short-grain rice
- 1 tablespoon olive oil
- 2 cups of water
- 1 teaspoon chili flakes
- 6 oz artichoke hearts, chopped
- ½ cup green peas
- 1 onion, sliced
- 1 cup bell pepper, sliced

Directions:

1. Pour water into the saucepan. Add rice and cook it for 15 mins.
2. Meanwhile, heat olive oil in the skillet.
3. Add chili flakes, dried saffron, onion, and bell pepper.
4. Roast the vegetables for 5 minutes.
5. Add them to the cooked rice.

6. Then add green peas and artichoke hearts. Toss the paella well and cook it for 10 minutes over low heat.

Per serving: 160 calories, 5.2g protein, 32.7g carbs, 2.7g fat, 3.2g fiber, 0mg cholesterol, 33mg sodium, 237mg potassium.

Mushroom Cakes

Preparation time: 15 min

Cooking time: 10 min

Servings: 4

Ingredients:

- 2 cups mushrooms, chopped
- 3 garlic cloves, chopped
- 1 tablespoon dried dill
- 1 egg, beaten
- ¼ cup of rice, cooked
- 1 tablespoon sesame oil
- 1 teaspoon chili powder

Directions:

1. Grind the mushrooms in the food processor.
2. Add egg, rice, garlic, dill and chili powder.
3. Blend the mixture for 10 seconds.
4. Then, heat up sesame oil for 1 minute.
5. Make the medium-sized mushroom cakes and put them in the hot sesame oil.
6. Cook the mushroom cakes for 10 minutes (about 5 minutes per side) on medium heat.

Per serving: 100 calories, 3.5g protein, 12g carbs, 4.8g fat, 0.9g fiber, 41mg cholesterol, 27mg sodium, 187mg potassium.

Glazed Eggplant Rings

Preparation time: 10 min

Cooking time: 10 min

Servings: 4

Ingredients:

- 3 eggplants, sliced
- 1 tablespoon liquid honey
- 1 teaspoon minced ginger
- 2 tablespoons lemon juice
- 3 tablespoons avocado oil
- ½ teaspoon ground coriander
- 3 tablespoons water

Directions:

1. Rub the eggplants with ground coriander.
2. Then heat the avocado oil in the skillet for 1 minute.
3. When the oil is very hot, add the sliced eggplant and arrange it in one layer.
4. Cook the vegetables for 2 minute per side.
5. Transfer the eggplant to the bowl.
6. Then add liquid honey, minced ginger, lemon juice, and water in the skillet.
7. Bring it to a boil and then add cooked eggplants.
8. Cover the vegetables in the sweet liquid well and cook for another 2 minutes.

Per serving: 130 calories, 3.3g protein, 29.6g carbs, 2.2g fat, 15.1g fiber, 0mg cholesterol, 11mg sodium, 993mg potassium.

Sweet Potato Balls

Preparation time: 15 min

Cooking time: 10 min

Servings: 4

Ingredients:

- 1 cup sweet potato, mashed, cooked
- 1 tablespoon fresh cilantro, chopped
- 1 egg, beaten
- 3 tablespoons ground oatmeal
- 1 teaspoon ground paprika
- ½ teaspoon ground turmeric
- 2 tablespoons coconut oil

Directions:

1. Mix up mashed sweet potato, paprika, fresh cilantro, egg, ground oatmeal, and turmeric in the bowl.
2. Toss the mixture until smooth and make the small balls.
3. Heat the coconut oil in the saucepan.
4. When the coconut oil is very hot, add the sweet potato balls.
5. Cook them until golden brown.

Per serving: 130 calories, 2.8g protein, 13.1g carbs, 8.2g fat, 2.2g fiber, 41mg cholesterol, 44mg sodium, 283mg potassium.

Chickpea Curry

Preparation time: 10 min

Cooking time: 10 min

Servings: 4

Ingredients:

- 1 ½ cup chickpeas, boiled
- 1 teaspoon curry powder
- ½ teaspoon garam masala
- 1 cup spinach, chopped
- 1 teaspoon coconut oil
- ¼ cup of soy milk
- 1 tablespoon tomato paste
- ½ cup of water

Directions:

1. Heat coconut oil in the saucepan.
2. Add tomato paste, curry powder, garam masala and soy milk.
3. Toss the mixture until smooth and bring it to a boil.
4. Add water, spinach, and chickpeas.
5. Stir the meal and close the lid.
6. Cook it for 5 minutes over medium-high heat.

Per serving: 278 calories, 16.4g protein, 47.8g carbs, 6.1g fat, 13.6g fiber, 0mg cholesterol, 37mg sodium, 765mg potassium.

Quinoa Bowl

Preparation time: 15 min

Cooking time: 15 min

Servings: 4

Ingredients:

- 1 cup quinoa
- 2 cups of water
- 1 cup tomatoes, diced
- 1 cup sweet pepper, diced
- ½ cup of rice, cooked
- 1 tablespoon lemon juice
- ½ teaspoon lemon zest, grated

- 1 tablespoon olive oil

Directions:

1. Mix up quinoa and water and cook it for 15 minutes. After this, remove it from the heat and leave it to rest for 10 minutes.
2. Transfer the cooked quinoa to the big bowl.
3. Add tomatoes, rice, lemon juice, sweet pepper, lemon zest, and olive oil.
4. Toss the mixture well and transfer it to the serving bowls.

Per serving: 270 calories, 9.4g protein, 48.9g carbs, 6.4g fat, 4.3g fiber, 0mg cholesterol, 11mg sodium, 435mg potassium.

Vegan Meatloaf

Preparation time: 10 min

Cooking time: 30 min

Servings: 6

Ingredients:

- 1 cup chickpeas, cooked
- 1 onion, diced
- 1 tablespoon ground flax seeds
- ½ teaspoon chili flakes
- 1 tablespoon coconut oil
- ½ cup carrot, diced
- ½ cup celery stalk, chopped
- 1 tablespoon tomato paste

Directions:

1. Heat coconut oil in the saucepan.
2. Add onion, carrot and celery stalk. Cook the vegetables for 10 minutes.
3. Then add chili flakes, chickpeas and ground flax seeds.
4. Blend the mixture until smooth with the immersion blender.
5. After this, line the loaf mold with baking paper and transfer the blended mixture inside.
6. Flatten well and spread with tomato paste.
7. Bake the meatloaf in the preheated to 365°F oven for 22 minutes.

Per serving: 182 calories, 7.1g protein, 23.9g carbs, 4.7g fat, 7g fiber, 0mg cholesterol, 25mg sodium, 407mg potassium.

Loaded Potato Skins

Preparation time: 15 min

Cooking time: 45 min

Servings: 6

Ingredients:

- 6 potatoes
- 1 teaspoon ground black pepper
- 2 tablespoons olive oil
- ½ teaspoon minced garlic
- ¼ cup of soy milk

Directions:

1. Preheat the oven to 400F.
2. Tickle the potatoes with the help of the fork 2-3 times and bake for 30 minutes or until vegetables are tender.
3. After this, cut the baked potatoes into halves and scoop out the potato meat in the bowl.
4. Drizzle the scooped potato halves with olive oil and ground black pepper and return to the oven. Bake them until they are light brown.

5. Then, mash the scooped potato meat and mix it up with soy milk and minced garlic.
6. Fill the cooked potato halves with mashed potato mixture.

Per serving: 190 calories, 4g protein, 34.4g carbs, 5.1g fat, 5.3g fiber, 0mg cholesterol, 18mg sodium, 884mg potassium.

Desserts

Sweet Fruit Salad

Preparation time: 10 min

Cooking time: 0 min

Servings: 2

Ingredients:

- ½ cup strawberries halves
- ½ cup grapes halved
- 4 oz mango, chopped
- ¼ cup fat-free yogurt
- 1 teaspoon lime zest, grated
- 1 tablespoon liquid honey

Directions:

1. In the salad bowl mix up strawberries, mango, grapes and lime zest.
2. Then add yogurt and drizzle the salad with liquid honey.
3. Stir gently.

Per serving: 115 calories, 2g protein, 26.4g carbs, 0.5g fat, 2g fiber, 1mg cholesterol, 25mg sodium, 279mg potassium.

Berry Sundae

Preparation time: 15 min

Servings: 6

Ingredients:

- 1 ½ cups coarsely chopped strawberries
- 1 ½ cups blueberries
- 1 ½ cups raspberries
- 1 ½ tablespoons balsamic vinegar
- Pinch of cracked black pepper
- 1 ½ teaspoons grated lemon zest
- 1 ½ teaspoons grated orange zest
- Juice of 1/2 orange
- ½ teaspoon vanilla extract
- 3 cups low-fat plain Greek yogurt
- 6 tablespoons sliced toasted almonds

Directions:

1. In a large pot over mid/high heat, put all the ingredients except the yogurt and almonds and cook until the liquid starts to bubble.
2. Reduce the heat to low and simmer for about 15 minutes, or until the mixture thickens. The berries will break apart spontaneously, leaving a mildly chunky sauce.
3. Mash the berries with a fork or masher for a smoother sauce. Remove yourself from the sun. In six cups, add 1/2 cup of yogurt and finish with sauce and toasted almonds.

Grilled Apricots with Cinnamon

Preparation time: 5 min

Servings: 6

Ingredients:

- 4 large apricots, halved and pitted
- 1 tablespoon extra-virgin olive oil
- ¼ teaspoon ground cinnamon

Directions:

1. Brush with oil on both sides of each apricot half, and put flat
2. On the hot grill or grill pan, side down. Grill for around 4 minutes, turn over the apricot halves and grill until soft for a few more

minutes. Sprinkle with cinnamon and cut the apricots from the grill. Enjoy being wet or cold.

Peaches with Ricotta Stuffing and Balsamic Glaze

Preparation time: 5 min

Servings: 4

Ingredients:

- 4 large peaches, halved and pitted
- 1 tablespoon extra-virgin olive oil
- 1 cup low-fat ricotta cheese
- ¼ teaspoon ground cinnamon
- 1/8 teaspoon ground nutmeg
- 2 tablespoons low-fat milk
- 2 tablespoons Balsamic Glaze

Directions:

1. Brush the two sides of each half of the peach with oil, and put them down. On the hot grill or grill pan, side down. Grill for about 4 minutes, turn over the peach halves and grill until soft for a few more minutes.
2. When the peaches are grilling, mix the ricotta, milk, cinnamon, and nutmeg in a small bowl, stirring evenly to combine flavors.
3. Take the peaches from the grill and add 1/4 cup of the ricotta mixture to the middle of each half of the peach. Drizzle and serve the balsamic glaze on each one.

Beans Brownies

Preparation time: 15 min

Cooking time: 15 min

Servings: 6

Ingredients:

- 1 cup black beans, cooked
- 1 tablespoon cocoa powder
- 5 oz quick oats
- 3 tablespoons of liquid honey
- 1 teaspoon baking powder
- 1 tablespoon lemon juice
- 1 teaspoon vanilla extract
- 1 teaspoon olive oil

Directions:

1. Mash black beans until smooth and stir with cocoa powder, honey, quick oats, baking powder, lemon juice, and vanilla extract.
2. Add olive oil and stir with the spoon.
3. Then, cover the baking pan with baking paper.
4. Transfer the brownie mixture to the baking tray and flatten it well. Cut the brownie into the bars.
5. Bake the dessert in the preheated to 360F oven for 15 minutes.
6. Cool the cooked brownies well.

Per serving: 244 calories,10.3g protein, 45.8g carbs, 2.9g fat, 7.6g fiber, 0mg cholesterol, 5mg sodium, 681mg potassium.

Avocado Mousse

Preparation time: 10 min

Cooking time: 0 min

Servings: 2

Ingredients:

- 1 avocado, peeled, pitted
- ½ cup low-fat milk
- 1 teaspoon vanilla extract
- 1 tablespoon cocoa powder
- 2 teaspoons liquid honey

Directions:

1. Chop avocado and put it in the food processor.
2. Add milk, vanilla extract, and cocoa powder.
3. Blend the mixture until smooth.
4. Pour the cooked mousse into the jar and top with honey.

Per serving: 260 calories, 4.5g protein, 19.2g carbs, 20.5g fat, 7.5g fiber, 3mg cholesterol, 34mg sodium, 653mg potassium.

Fruit Kebabs

Preparation time: 10 min

Cooking time: 0 min

Servings: 3

Ingredients:

- 1 cup strawberries
- 1 cup melon, cubed
- 1 cup grapes
- 2 kiwis, cubed
- 1 cup watermelon, cubed

Directions:

1. String the fruits in the wooden skewers one by one.
2. Put the cooked fruit kebabs in the fridge, for 30 minutes.

Per serving: 90 calories, 1.8g protein, 24.4g carbs, 0.7g fat, 3.4g fiber, 0mg cholesterol, 12mg sodium, 485mg potassium.

Vanilla Soufflé

Preparation time: 10 min

Cooking time: 30 min

Servings: 2

Ingredients:

- 2 egg yolks, whisked
- 2 tablespoons whole-grain wheat flour
- 1 teaspoon vanilla extract
- 1 tablespoon potato starch
- 2 tablespoons agave nectar
- 1 cup low-fat milk

Directions:

1. Mix up milk and egg yolks.
2. Add vanilla extract, flour, and potato starch.
3. Mix the liquid until smooth and bring it to a boil.
4. Add agave syrup and stir well.
5. Then spread the mixture into the soufflé ramekins and transfer them in the preheated to 350F oven.
6. Bake soufflé for 17 minutes.

Per serving: 149 calories, 7.8g protein, 12.9g carbs, 5.8g fat, 0.9g fiber, 216mg cholesterol, 62mg sodium, 235mg potassium.

Strawberries in Dark Chocolate

Preparation time: 15 min

Cooking time: 1 min

Servings: 2

Ingredients:

- 1 cup strawberries
- 1 tablespoon olive oil
- 1 oz dark chocolate, chopped

Directions:

1. Put the chocolate in the microwave oven for 30 seconds and melt it.
2. Then mix up olive oil and chocolate. Whisk well.
3. Freeze the strawberries for 15 minutes.
4. Then sprinkle them with a chocolate mixture.

Per serving: 149 calories, 1.6g protein, 14g carbs, 11.4g fat, 1.9g fiber, 3mg cholesterol, 12mg sodium, 163mg potassium.

Fruit Bowl

Preparation time: 10 min

Cooking time: 0 min

Servings: 4

Ingredients:

- 1 pitaya, peeled, chopped
- 2 kiwis, chopped
- 2 bananas, chopped
- ½ cup mango, chopped
- 1 teaspoon chia seeds
- 1 teaspoon coconut flakes

Directions:

1. Mix up bananas, pitaya, kiwis and mango in the big bowl.
2. Then transfer the mixture into the serving jar and spread with chia seeds and coconut flakes.

Per serving: 105 calories, 1.7g protein, 26.1g carbs, 1.3g fat, 3.9g fiber, 0mg cholesterol, 3mg sodium, 373mg potassium.

Grilled Pineapple

Preparation time: 5min

Servings: 6

Ingredients:

- 1 large pineapple, sliced into rounds and cored

Directions:

1. Laying it on its side and cutting the pineapple, cut the pineapple bottom and top. On its freshly flat frame, stand it up. Cut the skin off downward, beginning from the top and moving to the root, operating in a circular direction.
2. Be careful not to take too much of the skin off the fruit. Cut out any brown stains until the skin has been removed. Then lay it again lengthwise, and split the rounds to the thickness you like. Cut out the inedible

heart at the middle of each round with a cookie cutter or knife.
3. Place the rings directly on a hot grill with the pineapple. Grill for roughly three minutes or before char marks emerge. Switch the rings over, then barbecue for an extra 2 to 3 minutes. Serve chilled or hot.

Red Sangria

Preparation time: 5min

Servings: 8

Ingredients:

- 1 (750 mL) bottle Spanish red table wine
- ¼ cup brandy
- ¼ cup Cointreau
- ½ cup orange juice
- 1 cup pomegranate juice
- 2 oranges, thinly sliced
- 2 Granny Smith apples, thinly sliced
- 1 ½ cups seltzer, mineral water, or club soda

Directions:

1. Stir together the champagne, brandy, Cointreau, and fruit juices in a big pitcher.
2. Add the sliced fruit and chill for at least 30 minutes in the refrigerator before eating. Just before serving, add the seltzer, sparkling water, or club soda.

Baked Apples Stuffed with Cranberries and Walnuts

Preparation time: 30 Minutes

Servings: 4

Ingredients:

- Four baking apples, such as Braeburn or Rome ½ lemon
- ⅓ cup dried cranberries
- ⅓ cup chopped walnuts
- 6 tablespoons grade B maple syrup
- ¼ teaspoon ground cinnamon
- ¼ teaspoon freshly grated nutmeg
- 4 teaspoons unsalted butter
- 1 cup boiling water

Directions:

1. Preheat the oven to 350°F.
2. Break off the top inch of an apple one at a time to make a "lid." With a melon baller, scoop out the heart, stopping about half an inch from the bottom of the apple. Pick out the top half of the apple skin using a vegetable peeler. Rub the raw flesh with half of the lemon all over it.
3. Combine the cranberries, walnuts, 2 teaspoons of maple syrup, cinnamon, and nutmeg in a medium cup. Stuff the mixture into the apples. Top each one with 1 butter teaspoon. Replace the' lids of the fruit.'
4. To keep the apples, move to a baking dish only big enough. Squeeze half of the lemon juice from the lemon over the apples. Pour the boiling water in and securely cover it with aluminum foil. 20 minutes of baking. Uncover and baste with the liquid in the baking dish. Continue to bake until the apples are tender, 20 to 30 minutes longer, depending on the size of the apples when pierced with the tip of a small,

sharp knife. Take it out of the oven and let it stand for 5 minutes.
5. Move each apple to a dessert bowl and add 1 tablespoon of maple syrup each to drizzle. Serve it sweet.

Buttermilk Panna Cotta with Fresh Berries

Preparation time: 30 Minutes

Servings: 4

Ingredients:

- 3 teaspoons unflavored gelatin powder
- ¼ cup plus 2 tablespoons low-fat (1%) milk
- 2¾ cups buttermilk
- ½ cup amber agave nectar or honey
- ½ teaspoon vanilla extract
- Canola oil in a pump sprayer
- ½ cup fresh blueberries
- ½ cup fresh raspberries

Directions:

1. Sprinkle the gelatin in a small heatproof bowl over the milk and let stand until the milk is absorbed by the gelatin, for about 5 minutes. To get 1/2 inch up the sides, add enough water to a small skillet and bring it to a simmer over low-medium heat. Put the bowl in the water with the gelatin mixture and constantly stir with a small heatproof spatula until the gelatin melts and dissolves entirely around 2 minutes.
2. Meanwhile, over medium-low heat, heat the buttermilk in a medium saucepan, stirring continuously, only until it is warm to the touch. Do not overheat, or maybe it will curdle. Remove yourself from the sun. Attach the mixture of the gelatin and whisk until mixed. Agave and vanilla whisk. Transfer to a pitcher of liquid.
3. Oil six 6-ounce custard cups or ramekins. Pour the buttermilk mixture into the ramekins in equal quantities. Cover with plastic wrap for each one. Refrigerate for at least 5 h , or up to 2 days, until chilled and set.
4. Run a dinner knife around each ramekin's inside, making sure you hit bottom to crack the air seal. Place a dish over the top of the ramekin when working with one panna cotta at a time. Offer them a firm shake by holding the ramekin and dish together to unmold the panna cotta on the plate. Dip the ramekin (right side up) in a bowl of hot water and keep it for 10 seconds, dry the ramekin, invert, and try again to unmold. The blueberries and raspberries are sprinkled and served chilled.

Berry Smoothie

Preparation time: 5 min

Cooking time: 0 min

Servings: 2

Ingredients:

- 1 cup blackberries
- 1 cup strawberries
- 1 cup blueberries
- 1 cup low-fat yogurt

Directions:

1. Pour all ingredients in the mixer and blend until you get a smooth mixture.
2. Pour the cooked smoothie into the glasses.

Per serving: 177 calories, 9g protein, 30.6g carbs, 2.3g fat, 7g fiber, 7mg cholesterol, 88mg sodium, 569mg potassium.

Grilled Peaches

Preparation time: 10 min

Cooking time: 4 min

Servings: 4

Ingredients:

- 8 peaches, pitted, halved
- 1 teaspoon canola oil
- ½ teaspoon ground cinnamon

Directions:

1. Preheat the grill to 395F.
2. After this, sprinkle the peaches with ground cinnamon and canola oil.
3. Insert the fruits in the grill and roast them for 4 minutes (2 minutes per side).

Per serving: 119 calories, 2.8g protein, 28.2g carbs, 2g fat, 4.8g fiber, 0mg cholesterol, 0mg sodium, 571mg potassium.

Stuffed Fruits

Preparation time: 10 min

Cooking time: 0 min

Servings: 3

Ingredients:

- 3 figs, raw
- 3 teaspoons low-fat goat cheese
- 1 tablespoon liquid honey
- 3 walnuts

Directions:

1. Make the cross on the top of each fig and take a small amount of fig meat from them.
2. Then fill figs with low-fat goat cheese and walnuts.
3. Spread the fruits with liquid honey.

Per serving: 193 calories, 6g protein, 18g carbs, 11.9g fat, 2.9g fiber, 15mg cholesterol, 51mg sodium, 140mg potassium.

Oatmeal Cookies

Preparation time: 10 min

Cooking time: 15 min

Servings: 4

Ingredients:

- 1 cup oatmeal, grinded
- 1 teaspoon vanilla extract
- 1 teaspoon honey
- 3 bananas, mashed

Directions:

1. Mix up mashed bananas and oatmeal.
2. Add vanilla extract and honey. Stir the mixture well.
3. Then cover the baking tray with baking sheet.
4. Make small cookies with the banana mixture with the help of a spoon and place them in the prepared baking dish.
5. Bake the cookies for 15 minutes at 360°F until the cookies are light brown.

Per serving: 150 calories, 4g protein, 32g carbs, 1.6g fat, 4.4g fiber, 0mg cholesterol, 2mg sodium, 393mg potassium.

Baked Apples

Preparation time: 10 min

Cooking time: 35 min

Servings: 3

Ingredients:

- 3 apples
- 3 pecans, chopped
- 1 tablespoon raisins, chopped
- 3 teaspoons liquid honey
- ½ teaspoon ground cardamom

Directions:

1. Pick the tops of the apples to get the medium-sized holes.
2. Then fill the holes with raisins, pecans and ground cardamom.
3. Add honey and wrap the apples in the foil (separately - wrap each apple).
4. Bake the apples in the preheated to 380°F oven for 40 minutes.

Per serving: 240 calories, 2.3g protein, 42.2g carbs, 10.4g fat, 7.1g fiber, 0mg cholesterol, 3mg sodium, 327mg potassium.

Peach Crumble

Preparation time: 15 min

Cooking time: 25 min

Servings: 2

Ingredients:

- 1 cup peach, chopped
- 1 teaspoon ground nutmeg
- ½ teaspoon ground cinnamon
- 2 tablespoons margarine, softened
- 4 tablespoons oatmeal, grinded
- 1 teaspoon olive oil

Directions:

1. Mix up oatmeal and margarine. When you get a dough, crumble the mixture with the fingertips.
2. Then, brush the small baking pan with olive oil and put the peaches inside.
3. Spread the peaches with ground nutmeg and ground cinnamon.
4. Top the fruits with crumbled dough.
5. Bake the meal at 360°F until you get the light brown crust.

Per serving: 190 calories, 2.3g protein, 18.1g carbs, 15g fat, 2.7g fiber, 0mg cholesterol, 134mg sodium, 192mg potassium.

Cantaloupe and Mint Ice Pops

Preparation time: 30 Min

Servings: 4

Ingredients:

- 3 cups peeled, seeded, and cubed ripe cantaloupe
- ½ cup amber agave nectar
- 2 tablespoons fresh lemon juice
- 1 tablespoon finely chopped fresh mint

Directions:

1. Have eight ice pop molds ready. In a food processor or blender, purée 2 1/2 cups of cantaloupe cubes. Transfer to a bowl. Mix in the food processor or blender (or slice by hand) the remaining 1/2 cup of cantaloupe cubes until finely chopped, and add to the puree. Apply the agave, lemon juice, and mint to the whisk.
2. Divide the puree between the ice pop molds and cover the lid of each mold. Freeze for at least 4 hours until the pops are strong. (The pops can be kept in the freezer for up to 1 week.)
3. Rinse the pop mold under lukewarm water to serve, then remove the pop from the mold. Frozen serve.
4. Cantaloupe and Mint Granita: Put a metal baking dish or cake pan and a metal fork until very cold, approximately 15 minutes, in the freezer. The whole cantaloupe puree. To combine well, add the agave and the lemon juice and pulse. Only to mix, add the mint and pulse. Pour into the metal dish and freeze for around 1 hour until the mixture is icy along the sides of the bowl. Stir the ice crystals into the middle using the cold fork. Freeze again, around 1 hour more, until frosty, and stir again; the mixture becomes more solid. Freeze for about 1 hour more until the consistency is slushy. Freeze for up to 4 hours before serving. Using the fork's tines to scrape the mixture into frozen slush just before serving. Serve in chilled bowls immediately.

Peach and Granola Parfaits

Preparation time: 30 min

Servings: 4

Ingredients:

- 1 cup plain low-fat Greek yogurt
- 2 tablespoons amber agave nectar, honey, or grade B maple syrup
- 1/4 teaspoon vanilla extract
- 8 tablespoons Make It Your Way Granola
- 4 ripe peaches or nectarines, pitted and cut into 1/2-inch dice

Directions:

1. Stir the yogurt, agave, and vanilla in a small cup.
2. Layer 1 tablespoon of granola, 2 tablespoons of yogurt, and one-eighth of the diced peaches in a large parfait glass or wineglass for each serving, then repeat again. Immediately serve.

Banana Saute

Preparation time: 5 min

Cooking time: 5 min

Servings: 2

Ingredients:

- 2 bananas, peeled
- 2 tablespoons orange juice
- 1 tablespoon margarine

Directions:

1. Slice the bananas lengthwise.
2. Put the margarine in the skillet and melt it.
3. Pour the sliced bananas in the hot margarine and drizzle with orange juice.
4. Sautèe the fruits for 4 minutes (2 minutes per side) on medium heat.

Per serving: 160 calories, 4g protein, 30.6g carbs, 6.1g fat, 3.1g fiber, 0mg cholesterol, 68mg sodium, 456mg potassium.

Rhubarb Muffins

Preparation time: 10 min

Cooking time: 15 min

Servings: 4

Ingredients:

- 1 cup rhubarb, diced
- ¼ cup applesauce
- 1 egg, beaten
- 1 teaspoon baking powder
- 1 cup whole-wheat flour
- 1 tablespoon avocado oil
- 1 teaspoon lemon zest, grated
- ½ cup low-fat yogurt
- 2 tablespoons of liquid honey

Directions:

1. Toss applesauce, egg, flour, baking powder, avocado oil, lemon zest, honey, and yogurt in the mixing bowl.
2. When you get the smooth texture, add rhubarb and stir it well with the spoon.
3. Preheat the oven to 365°F.
4. Fill 1/3 part of every muffin mold with rhubarb batter and transfer them to the oven.
5. Bake the muffins for 18 minutes.

Per serving: 220 calories, 6.7g protein, 37.8g carbs, 2.3g fat, 1.8g fiber, 43mg cholesterol, 41mg sodium, 363mg potassium.

Poached Pears

Preparation time: 5 min

Cooking time: 35 min

Servings: 6

Ingredients:

- 6 pears, peeled
- 3 cups orange juice
- 1 teaspoon cardamom
- 1 cinnamon stick
- 1 anise star

Directions:

1. In the skillet, mix up orange juice, cinnamon stick, cardamom, and anise star.
2. Bring the liquid to a boil.
3. Add peeled pears and close the lid.

4. Cook the fruits for 25 minutes on medium heat.

Per serving: 158 calories, 2g protein, 55g carbs, 0.6g fat, 6.8g fiber, 0mg cholesterol, 4mg sodium, 494mg potassium.

Lemon Pie

Preparation time: 15 min

Cooking time: 15 min

Servings: 8

Ingredients:

- 1 pie crust
- ¼ cup lemon juice
- ½ cup low-fat milk
- 3 egg yolks
- 2 tablespoons potato starch

Directions:

1. Pour milk into the saucepan.
2. Add starch, egg yolks, and lemon juice.
3. Whisk the liquid until smooth.
4. Simmer it for 6 minutes. Stir it constantly.
5. Then leave the mixture for 20 minutes to chilling.
6. Pour the lemon mix over the pie-crust and flatten it well.

Per serving: 179 calories, 4g protein, 23.9g carbs, 9.3g fat, 0.5g fiber, 79mg cholesterol, 182mg sodium, 66mg potassium.

Fresh Strawberries with Chocolate Dip

Preparation time: 30 min

Servings: 4

Ingredients:

- ½ cup low-fat (2%) canned evaporated milk
- 5 ounces bittersweet chocolate (about 60% cacao content), finely chopped
- 24 strawberries, unhulled

Directions:

1. In a tiny saucepan, carry the evaporated milk to a boil over medium heat. Remove from the heat and then, add the chocolate. Let it stand for about 3 minutes before the chocolate softens. Until smooth, whisk.
2. Divide the mixture of chocolate into four tiny ramekins. To dip, serve the strawberries with the chocolate mixture.

Cardamom Pudding

Preparation time: 20 min

Cooking time: 10 min

Servings: 2

Ingredients:

- 1 cup of coconut milk
- 1 teaspoon agar agar
- 1 teaspoon ground cardamom
- 1 teaspoon vanilla extract
- 1 teaspoon honey

Directions:

1. Pour coconut milk into the saucepan.
2. Add agar, ground cardamom, and vanilla extract. Whisk the liquid until smooth.
3. Bring it to a boil and simmer for 5 minutes on low heat.

4. Remove the pudding from heat and chilling for 20 minutes.
5. Add honey and stir well.
6. Transfer the pudding to the serving cups and leave it for 10 minutes in the fridge.

Per serving: 288 calories, 4g protein, 9g carbs, 28.7g fat, 3.1g fiber, 0mg cholesterol, 20mg sodium, 333mg potassium.

Banana Bread

Preparation time: 15 min

Cooking time: 45 min

Servings: 6

Ingredients:

- ½ cup low-fat sour cream
- 2 bananas, mashed
- 1 teaspoon baking powder
- 1 teaspoon apple cider vinegar
- 1 egg, beaten
- ½ cup oatmeal, grinded
- ¼ cup whole-wheat flour
- 2 tablespoons margarine, melted

Directions:

1. Toss all ingredients and whisk the mixture until smooth.
2. Then preheat the oven to 360°F.
3. Put the banana bread mixture into the loaf mold and flatten well.
4. Bake the banana-bread in the oven for 50 minutes.
5. Chill the cooked bread well, remove it from the loaf-mold and slice into the servings.

Per serving: 174 calories, 4g protein, 20.9g carbs, 9.2g fat, 1.9g fiber, 36mg cholesterol, 66mg sodium, 295mg potassium.

Made in United States
Orlando, FL
16 January 2022